THE UNIVERSITY OF NORTH CAROLINA
SOCIAL STUDY SERIES

SOCIAL WORK

And the Training of

SOCIAL WORKERS

THE UNIVERSITY OF NORTH CAROLINA
SOCIAL STUDY SERIES

ODUM AND JOHNSON: *The Negro and His Songs* . .	$3.00
PUCKETT: *Folk Beliefs of the Southern Negro* . . .	5.00
ODUM AND JOHNSON: *Negro Workaday Songs* . . .	3.00
ODUM AND OTHERS: *Southern Pioneers*	2.00
POUND: *Law and Morals*	2.00
GIDDINGS: *The Scientific Study of Human Society* . .	2.00
ODUM AND WILLARD: *Systems of Public Welfare* . .	2.00
BRANSON: *Farm Life Abroad*	2.00
ROSS: *Roads to Social Peace*	1.50
WILLEY: *The Country Newspaper*	1.50
JORDAN: *Children's Interest in Reading*	1.50
ODUM: *An Approach to Public Welfare and Social Work*	1.50
NORTH: *Social Differentiation*	2.50
KNIGHT: *Among the Danes*	2.50
STEINER AND BROWN: *The North Carolina Chain Gang*	2.00
LOU: *Juvenile Courts in the United States*	3.00
CARTER: *Social Theories of L. T. Hobhouse* . . .	1.50
BROWN: *A State Movement in Railroad Development* .	5.00
MILLER: *Town and County*	2.00
MITCHELL: *William Gregg, Factory Master of the Old South*	3.00
METFESSEL: *Phonophotography in Folk Music* . .	3.00
WAGER: *County Government in North Carolina* . .	5.00
WALKER: *Social Work and the Training of Social Workers*	2.00

THE UNIVERSITY OF NORTH CAROLINA PRESS
CHAPEL HILL, N. C.

THE BAKER AND TAYLOR CO.
NEW YORK

OXFORD UNIVERSITY PRESS
LONDON

MARUZEN-KABUSHIKI-KAISHA
TOKYO

SOCIAL WORK
AND THE TRAINING OF
SOCIAL WORKERS

By

SYDNOR H. WALKER

CHAPEL HILL
THE UNIVERSITY OF NORTH CAROLINA PRESS
1928

PRINTED IN THE UNITED STATES OF AMERICA
BY EDWARDS & BROUGHTON COMPANY, RALEIGH, N. C.

THIS BOOK WAS DIGITALLY PRINTED.

PREFACE

THIS study was made in the belief that a lay opinion upon social work and the education of social workers might have certain advantages in interpreting these enterprises to a non-professional group. The writer has had the experience neither of being a social worker nor of instructing social workers, but has acted upon the assumption that perspective gained from an outside point of view may balance these deficiencies.

In the course of this survey most of the schools of social work in the United States and Canada were visited. Through attending the National Conferences for Social Work, talking with staff members of social agencies in all parts of the country, and reading the literature of this field, an idea of the philosophy and problems of social work was built up. In the discussion which follows, it should be clearly understood that statements refer only to conditions in the United States and Canada.

There are extenuating circumstances in any effort to illumine the subject of social work. So little has been written about its general assumptions and implications that there should be gain if a sincere approach is made from any angle. The writer seeks to stimulate discussion and enlightened consideration of the function of social work in contemporary society. In the following essay no final word is said upon any of the questions raised.

Grateful acknowledgment is made to Professor Henry R. Seager of Columbia University, to Beardsley Ruml, Edmund E. Day, and Lawrence K. Frank for their interest and counsel in the writing of this book. Professor Howard W. Odum and Professor Charles E. Merriam read the manuscript and made valuable suggestions which have been incorporated in the work as now presented.

SYDNOR H. WALKER

NEW YORK
May, 1928

TABLE OF CONTENTS

culty in distinguishing between public and private welfare work—No satisfactory estimates of totals—Support of welfare activities largely on public funds—Overlapping exists between public and private services—Survey of publicly administered welfare work greatly needed—Social work has several economic implications—Little to indicate social work can be self-supporting.

Social work an accepted part of social system—Point of view determines what social problems are—Unfortunate incidence of industrial system partially responsible for both ignorance and ill health—Social work seeks to adjust individuals and groups to their environment and to improve conditions which make adjustment difficult—Constructive work for normal population not commonly thought part of welfare program—Social workers appear to compromise with present system—Progress made in handling immediate relief problems since 1900—Consistent support given social and industrial legislation by social workers—Effort to meet existing evils as yet ineffective.

Seeks to coördinate various programs promoting human welfare—Carries on independent activities—Is social work a vocation with exclusive problems?—Has it a technique requiring special educational preparation?—Utilization of full community resources for benefit of clients is function exclusive to social work—Social worker the logical person to extend advisory service.

Primary claims for public support reflected in literature and official statements—Probably social work

not yet in position to be explained—Ability claimed
to influence human behavior through case work—
Case work implies more than counseling upon use
of community resources—Aspiration to professional
status rested upon asserted creation of unique technique—Case work an art, not science, as now prac-
ticed—Schools of social work of recent origin—
Russell Sage Foundation data upon educational
and professional training—Activities of case worker
not unlike those of others seeking to modify human
behavior—Good case work of great value—Not
more essential than assembling of data upon community—Consultants upon community resources
identified with social work.

Type of personnel determines quality and scope of
social work—No common denominator in character
of activities—Administration and organization of
social agencies, case work, and group work are central activities—Characteristics of social workers—
Salary level of social work too low—Range of
salaries narrow—Concentration of social workers
in cities—Case work leading activity—Research
and training command highest salaries—Public
skeptical about entrusting larger responsibilities—
Little done to make improvement in personnel
possible—Question of salaries crucial in determining personnel.

Specialized educational preparation for social work
essential—Present provisions far from satisfactory
—Preparation concentrates upon activities of essential nature, capable of description—Academic
preparation important only within past ten years—
Majority social workers product of apprenticeship

method—Prevalence of apprenticeship largely due to economic reasons—Some question superiority of academic training—Weight of argument now favors specialized education—Schools responsive to practical demands of field—Preparation for a number of important social welfare activities nowhere provided—Understanding between workers in public and private organizations essential—Schools must assume wider functions.

Chief interest centers in schools as group—Definite trend towards university affiliation—Varying admission requirements—Educators prefer graduate course—Suitability of subject matter to undergraduate college main point at issue—Social case work courses most numerous—Other technical courses involve application of case technique—Many courses contain no technical material—Field work makes largest time demands—Feasibility of undergraduate instruction depends upon practical questions—Insufficient experiment to prove undergraduate training, as such, successful or unsuccessful—Differentiated preparation for social work may be desirable—Education for social work regarded as legitimate university activity in few places—Association of Schools of Professional Social Work includes both graduate and undergraduate schools—Difficult to evaluate effect of schools upon field—Association not now an active organization.

Development has been independent—Each of the social sciences has roots in distant past—Sociology seeks to effect synthesis of social aspects of various sciences—Social work and social sciences now occupying adjacent territory—Social workers claim relationship—Are not equipped to apply data of social sciences—Are often critical of social scientists —Social scientists show slight interest in social work—Social science seeks to devise effective techniques—Deprecates claims that present social techniques are scientific—Relation of social worker to scientist that of technician to adviser—Responsibility of social workers to collect data in form usable for science—Strong public pressure upon scientists to study social problems—Application of laboratory methods presents great difficulties in social science—Valuable results anticipated from intimate contact with concrete social situations— Desired rapprochement between social scientists and social workers may be achieved—Coöperative research of great value to be anticipated—Program of social welfare then possible—Developments in social science will determine destiny of social work.

SOCIAL WORK

And the Training of

SOCIAL WORKERS

I

THE PRACTICAL BASIS OF SOCIAL WORK

THE basis of social work today is eminently practical. There are a large number of individuals in distress who seem incapable of solving their problems without help from the social group. Account must be taken of them and of their families, else the welfare of the community is threatened. Self-preservation as well as the spirit of humanity requires that the well-being of all members of society be set as a goal. Otherwise, the rate of social progress is slackened.

Such appears to be the philosophy of today, and yet there is no marked diminution in the number of those in distress. Why are there so many, singly or in groups, requiring help? Why is the aid given by society so ineffective in preventing the recurrence of the ills which overwhelm its individual members? The existence of persistent, deep-seated social evils is implied. These evils must be studied in some detail if there is to be understanding of the specific difficulties society is facing.

The majority of citizens, if asked to explain the fact that a certain individual is in trouble and needs help, would readily diagnose the case as "it's his own fault" or "he's the victim of circumstances." Neither of these answers would be greatly illuminating or dependable; yet they reflect in thoughtless fashion the causes of individual misfortune commonly recognized. Personal defect and unfavorable environment are the two general categories under which an infinite list of specific human ills is classified. Which of these two tags best applies in a particular case is largely a matter of opinion. The subject is as controversial as the related topic: Is heredity or environment the more important in conditioning the individual? A decision to use one tag rather than another to designate the original cause of an individual's difficulties is apt to be based on guesswork. The various elements which combine to create a given situation are so complex that a complete and thorough analysis of them leads away from decisive statement as to exact causes. Certainly, a real understanding of the situation will seldom result in finding either personal defect or environment alone responsible for producing the situation. Nor does the use of such general terms as "personal defect" and "unfavorable environment" advance us far toward an understanding of maladjustment. What kind of personal defect in combination with what kind of environment gives the key to an individual problem? Seldom is there any possibility of distinguishing sharply between the effects of a personal defect and the effects of an unfavorable environment. Bad environment produces physical and mental disabilities; personal defects may inevitably bring about an environment producing further disintegration. Where the trouble began, and what are the direct and indirect results of it, cannot be categorically stated.

It is useful, however, to list the factors which are present in a large number of cases of maladjustment. Though it may be impossible to say that a certain combination of personal traits and environmental conditions will inevitably cause maladjustment of a certain kind, recognition of the frequency of certain results in the presence of known factors is of value. No one should be so rash as to predict that a child who is blind, deaf, and dumb from birth will never become self-supporting; but it is clearly demonstrated from experience that considerable time and effort must be devoted to enable him to achieve a normal social life. The man who has been a criminal for fifteen years may begin a new career and becomes a responsible member of society. Usually, such a life has created an individual of fixed attitude against the social group, unlikely to change into a model citizen.

The quality of individual character may always arise to refute any assertion concerning the effect of a given list of misfortunes. One person goes down under one kind of trouble which another could withstand. The latter is, in turn, rendered helpless by a different calamity. A third man may rise above both these misfortunes and fall victim to a new ill which, in common opinion, is of less serious nature. To some, economic failure is a cause of disintegration; to others, it is ill-health; to still others, personal unhappiness and disillusionment are insurmountable.

Recognizing the capacity of individual character to triumph over great odds and to refute all predictions as to probable reactions in given situations, statements may still be made which shed light upon the causes of a large number of human failures. It is well known that certain conditions are more conducive to failure than others. What are these conditions, and why do they exist?

A first set of unfavorable conditions is found within the individual himself. Physical disabilities of all kinds —a defective mentality, a crippled body, a deficiency in sight, hearing, speaking—limit the possibilities of adjustment to the social group by the individual. Unless a specialized type of education and environment is provided for those ill-equipped physically and mentally, maladjustment is practically inevitable. Ordinary living may never be possible for the severely handicapped, but an ordered life with certain satisfactions can be provided when society recognizes its responsibility towards these persons who cannot solve their own problems. Today society accepts this charge of caring for persons with defects and afflictions. A large item in budgets of public welfare is usually devoted to this purpose. Few question the necessity of public provision for those whose handicaps are of a physical nature. Sympathy and initiative can be aroused when a definite need of further provisions for this group is discovered.

Provisions for rehabilitating individuals whose physical disabilities are acquired in the course of an active normal life are not as adequate as provisions for those who are born with defects, or who acquire them in childhood. The sense of public obligation lessens, apparently, when the individual is felt to be wholly or partially responsible for his own misfortune.

Other groups for whom there is inadequate public care are those whose physical and mental weaknesses are of rather indefinite nature. Complex principles are involved if public responsibility is assumed for those who do not seem up to par physically and mentally, or who seem a little dangerous and eccentric. Society has learned to make distinctions between those who are insane and those who are of evil intent, between those who are suffering from hookworm and those who are shiftless and irresponsible. There are methods for treating the insane and those suffering from known disease, but there are few dependable facts upon which to base a technique for handling the delinquent and the ineffective. In fact, a reliable method of picking out those who are likely to commit overt acts against the community has yet to be developed, and, if there were such a method, the determination of policies for handling such persons would be a difficult matter. Are there enough normal people willing and able to bear the load of a program which would make proper provision for all persons held to be, or likely to become, non-social? In what does proper provision consist?

A study of the present trend in public expenditures for care of defectives and delinquents should engender caution in urging the acceptance of broader responsibilities by the state. The State Controller of New York recently estimated that institutional facilities for the wards of the State would have to be doubled within the next thirty years if the present rate of increase of inmates is maintained. The cost of such an expansion would be about half a billion dollars. This estimate includes provision for individuals of the types already under institutional care. Present facilities for the feeble-minded are very limited; no more adequate provision for them is contemplated in this estimate and no new groups are considered.[1]

[1] *New York Times*, Feb. 5, 1928.

A large share of maladjustment today is evidently
due to physical and mental defects for which successful
treatment either cannot be, or is not, provided.
Whether it is feasible for society to attempt the cure
or treatment of all those suffering from physical and
mental defect is very doubtful. A more hopeful method
of meeting the situation appears to lie in the prevention
of physical and mental defects in so far as possible.

Nothing has yet been said to indicate why individuals are handicapped by physical defects which
render their social adjustment difficult. It is impossible
at times to say whether the defect was present at birth
or whether it resulted from the particular conditions
of infancy and childhood. The physical defects present
at birth could be prevented in large part by making it
impossible for the physically and mentally unfit to
reproduce, and by proper instruction of parents in
physical hygiene. In the United States today little
experiment in pushing either of these measures has
been attempted. To increasing degree, public support
is given to health and sanitation programs, but social
and ethical considerations prevent any whole-hearted
measures "to regulate private lives." The cost to the
state and to the individual of the policy of non-
interference is incalculable.

When the discussion turns to those physical and
mental handicaps which grow out of, or are complicated
by, social environment, there lies the territory which
should be most liable to improvement through a social
program. How many of the maladjusted have been
downed by the circumstances of their lives? How
possible is it to change these circumstances? Again,

here are questions to which it is impossible to make concise and convincing answer. But there need be no hesitancy in asserting that circumstances play a very important part in causing maladjustment and that definite suggestions for changing these circumstances can be made. Not only are physical handicaps made more onerous, but physical weakness and non-social attitudes are created by unfavorable environment.

"Unfavorable circumstances of life" is a term used to cover almost any situation in which an individual has failed to make a satisfactory adjustment. There are certain elements to be generally advocated in the surroundings of every individual; their absence may be termed, in general, unfavorable. These desired elements are a pleasant home, fresh air, sunshine, abundant pure water, wholesome food, healthy recreation, human affection, educational opportunities, congenial occupation, security, and participation in a community life. Other items might be substituted or added to those mentioned, but the essentials of a satisfying life are implied. An effort to check such a list as constants in the lives of those who are maladjusted would be revealing.

How large a portion of the population enjoys the advantages named? In modern cities few but the wealthy can afford pleasant homes with air and sunshine. If there is employment for the wage-earners of the family, food is not scarce though perhaps ill-balanced. Recreation of a sort is present in cities; often it becomes a source of demoralization. Human affection is too uncertain a quantity to permit any generalization as to its presence or absence. Educational opportunities are available in varying degree in the United States. Immigrants, illiterate adults, the colored races, the rural population have facilities very inferior to those offered the American-born white living in a city. The three last-mentioned elements suggested as desirable—congenial occupation, security, and community activity—are more often absent than present.

The absence of elements known to be favorable in the lives of many individuals requires some explanation. If it is agreed that the presence of a favorable environment—as just defined—will do much to prevent maladjustment due to physical and mental weakness and to non-social attitude, why does not the social group direct specific efforts towards the creation of such an environment? The answer is that a small number of intelligent and disinterested persons are making such an effort, but that their program is limited by lack of authority and by lack of financing on the one hand, by the weight of ignorance and vested interests on the other hand. The majority of people seem to believe that extreme poverty, disease, ignorance, moral turpitude will always be present to some degree in any society. Nor are they interested in experimenting with the possible variations to be rung upon the phrase "to some degree." It is argued that programs for better housing, recreation, public health, vocational training must wait upon the release of funds from their present use in meeting existing crises. If the New York State Controller's estimates are to be accepted, no funds are likely to be released at an early date from caring for those who are definitely out of adjustment.

Undoubtedly, money must be found to finance constructive programs in improving human environment, but much could be done with present facilities and without resort to public funds. In the matter of housing, the state through legislation can assure decent living quarters to many—and this without eliminating necessary profit to the landlord. Further, the state, through a levy upon industry, for the establishment of compensation and old age insurance funds, can prevent the destitution which follows the industrial injury or old age of the wage earner. Education for a vocation should be available to each child through the public schools already existing, and should furnish the background for intelligent choice of a life work. Provision for healthy recreation may be achieved partly through more intelligent use of public parks, museums, libraries, reservations, partly through the addition of publicly supported entertainment facilities of new kinds, and partly through regulation of commercialized recreation. Opportunity for the individual to participate in community life should grow out of a satisfactory recreational and educational program.

Provision for security is not easy to effect in complex modern society. Economic security, upon which other types of security largely depend, is notably lacking. The worker of today is able only to limited extent to control his earning power or his period of employment by efforts he himself makes. Factory production, specialized labor, and division of labor mean that the factory employee is relatively incapable of determining his wages on the basis of the efforts he himself makes. His wages depend upon the success of the business as a whole, and this success depends upon efficient management and public demand for goods as well as upon the productivity of the workers. Management must provide adequate capital, up-to-date machinery, efficient advertising, and advantageous marketing. Even then success is not assured if public demand is diverted to a new or competitive product. Unemployment may descend not only upon a factory, but also upon an industry, when, for instance, public taste prefers silk to cotton or woolen goods. While Mr. Ford decided with what new model he could successfully meet the competition of the automobile world, a large part of the working population of Detroit was denied employment.

Thus, not only is the amount of wages which the laborer earns largely outside his control, but opportunity to work is not a certainty. Individual skill in producing goods of certain quality and amount is only one factor in determining the price of the product, and, therefore, the wage level; the desire of the worker to be employed is only a small factor in securing him employment. The result of this state of affairs may be either low or high wages, either employment or unemployment, regardless of the worker's efforts or capacities.

The farmer is supposedly more independent than the industrial worker, since he is his own employer, owns the tools with which he works, and markets his products himself. He appears to control his conditions of work, but in reality his income is as precarious—maybe more so—than that of the worker in commerce or industry. Since the weather determines what his crop will be and world conditions determine what price his crop will bring, the amount of his income is very uncertain. His good crop may not be highly remunerative if there are good crops elsewhere and if demand does not increase with increased supply.

The miner, like the farmer and the industrial worker, cannot determine his income nor count on employment through his ability to produce a certain amount of coal each day. The world situation as to the demand for, and supply of, coal will be chiefly instrumental in fixing his wages and in giving or denying him employment. The industrial worker, the farmer, and the miner may alike be unable to make a living due to conditions outside their control. Each suffers from relative immobility—as compared with capital—in transferring his activities to a more remunerative occupation. Of the three, the industrial worker is probably the most mobile.

Lack of complete mobility in shifting occupation may be a temporary cause of unemployment and so of distress for the industrial worker; at the same time, the general mobility of labor may itself be a contributing cause to distress. The worker moves from plant to plant, from town to town, and from industry to industry, to take advantage of favorable wage rates. He puts down few roots and establishes few connections which give him a hold upon the community when ill-fortune overtakes him. His mobility, while incomplete, may be marked enough to prevent his identification with any group or with any community. The dislocations resulting from a cut in wages or unemployment may not be permanent, but a margin of time and of financial reserves is required for readjustment. Often the worker has been living at such low level that no reserves have been accumulated. Also, guidance may be needed in finding new work even when no financial difficulty exists.

Economic insecurity is enhanced by lack of general education and of specialized vocational training. Education, like social work, seeks to guide the individual to a satisfying life. In many cases it fails. It must struggle against the ills of bad heredity and environment, as well as against the uncertainty of its own objectives. Granted that children are to be trained for existing jobs, what are the requirements of those jobs, and to what do they lead? Careful analyses of vocations, of supply and of demand for workers and wage scales within various occupations, of probable lines of promotion, and of necessary personal qualifications for success are far from adequate. The placing of young people in positions is usually left to the workings of chance and to commercial employment offices. That there should be vocational misfits is not surprising. Too few remain in school long enough to be prepared for their life work—even supposing that the schools know how to give such preparation. A high school education does not assure those who graduate from it an escape from routinized or blind-alley work. Even college men with no vocational training find themselves with little choice as to vocation if they are forced to earn a living.

Often education solves the problem for those who have a definite idea as to what they want to do, the personal qualities which are requisite, and the opportunities which give necessary training. But the main difficulty lies in the fact that few persons have clearcut ideas about what they want to do or can do, and are apt to fall into jobs which are not educational. The general adoption of standardized methods in all departments of economic life—industry, commerce, and business—creates a need for a large army of routine workers. Men of originality, initiative, and high intellectual ability are needed to direct these workers, but the places requiring such qualities are few when compared with the number of routine jobs. The majority of workers, having no unusual qualities in the beginning, develop none on the job and lose whatever creative impulses and enthusiasm they may have. If the individual can persevere through routine jobs and can submerge his individuality temporarily without losing it, he may later win a place which will allow him to create and to develop. Too often a man continues on a single machine, performing one process in making a small part of an article. Or he becomes an adept in operating an adding machine or making out bills of lading. No idea of related processes or of the occupation as a whole is acquired, however long he performs his particular task.

Unemployment and low or irregular wages are not necessarily the consequences of routine work, of the subordination of the individual worker, and of the mechanization of life. Unfortunately they appear to be concomitants of industrial organization at many times and in many places. But denial of economic security and peace of mind seems inevitably to follow upon conditions which preclude the individual's controlling his means of livelihood. The uncertainty of his future may lead both to disintegration and to irresponsibility.

Many of those who need help in adjusting themselves are victims of an unsatisfactory economic status. Unemployment, low or irregular wages may mean poor living conditions, with illness, dependency, desertion, drunkenness, delinquency, and crime as direct or indirect results. And, in turn, poor environment may mean future low earning power, which indefinitely postpones any solution of the problem. Environment modifies, corrects, or destroys much that heredity bestows, and economic factors are of primary importance in shaping environment. Hence, a sound adjustment of society's ills must depend to marked degree upon a sound economic structure. Inventions, social habits, traditions, culture, physical heritage determine what this economic structure is; so there is no end or beginning in fixing responsibility.

Some remedies for economic insecurity are suggested by the enumeration of the factors which cause it. The individual must receive a broad vocational training while in school; he must shape this training to fit his general objectives in life. Industry on its side must solve the problem of equalizing production throughout the year and of shifting men when processes change. Prevention, when possible, of accidents and disease due to industry, and insurance against unavoidable disability are salutary measures capable of great extension.

A large number of individuals, presenting acute problems of maladjustment, are not apparently suffering primarily from physical or environmental handicaps which can be readily diagnosed. While it is possible that more refined methods of detecting such defects and measuring their influence will change the diagnosis, at the present time many individuals are said to be out of adjustment because of their social attitude. How such an attitude developed can be learned only by careful study of each personality; the effects of bad heredity, unfavorable environment, and physical mishaps may be compounded in the present attitude, and treatment may involve a modification of physical conditions. A sense of impotence or of futility, which can be traced to unsatisfactory economic status, may be overcome by finding congenial work. Maladjustment due to disillusionment, to lack of incentive to strive for a satisfying life, offers a challenge to those who believe that despair is the product of ignorance.

The social attitudes to be combatted are not all of negative quality. The delinquent and the criminal present cases of maladjustment which have taken the form of positive attitudes against society. Their reaction to an unsatisfactory environment has been revolt, a denial of the power of social sanctions to control them. It is important in discussing criminality to recognize that two factors enter in—the laws made by society, and the offender. Certain acts are labeled "crime" because they are contrary to the general social interest. The Volstead Act has created a large class of criminals in the eyes of the law, since individuals who buy or sell alcoholic beverages have been outlawed. Yet the act of buying or selling liquor is essentially the same act which, before 1919, was not regarded as criminal in the United States and still is not criminal in most countries of the world. Other regulations, which apply to automobile traffic, to housing, to censorship of literature and the drama, to public morality are built upon specific interests of a particular time and place. Yet those who go counter to such regulations commit a crime.

Much of juvenile delinquency is recognized as due to the natural impulses of youth finding no suitable outlet in the environment imposed by modern cities. It is difficult to show why certain things, which are not wrong in themselves, are wrong under the circumstances which social life necessitates. Still, individuals who resist man-made rules and assert their own interests are considered non-social and, in fact, often do the group as much harm as though they deliberately set out to cause trouble.

The melancholics, the malcontents, the family deserters, the drunkards, and the criminals are un-adjusted persons for whom society has found no place and who are unable to make a place for themselves. The result is that they break with society or society breaks with them. Men are not criminals by instinct, or through necessity, as is sometimes asserted, but are criminals because they possess personalities which are not adjusted to the environment in which they are placed. A certain kind of environment, as well as a certain type of personality, is instrumental in making a criminal.

How can such people be made to fit in and to believe that their real chance for a satisfying life is to accept the rulings and customs of the society in which they live? There is no answer to this question, since no one has yet produced a general or a specific formula for happiness. Furthermore, is it desirable that there should be general acceptance of life as it is? If the decision were unanimous among all intelligent people that the present is a well-ordered and satisfactory period in which to live, no fundamental change being advocated, a type of education which would train citizens to perpetuate the present might evolve. But the majority of the intelligent believe in progress and are unwilling to admit that something better than the present cannot be achieved. So, education falters in stating its purpose, and often only succeeds in turning out citizens who are resentful of the present and yet are not equipped to shape a different future.

The more complex our social life, the more complex are the social relationships resulting. A natural corollary is maladjustment. It is a recent development for man to work under conditions where his movements are routinized and endlessly repetitive; to use only one set of faculties over and over while other faculties are never exercised; to have all amusements and recreations of a commercialized kind which render the onlooker passive; to live in a cell among other cells where the identity of the individual seems blotted out. These conditions are judged abnormal by the adult generation which has known quite recently a somewhat different life. And because adults have ideas, fixed by an earlier set of conditions, they interfere with possible adjustments which their children might make to present conditions. Some doubt exists, moreover, as to the possibility of satisfactory life under the conditions described, even if there were no mental or emotional resistance. Can individuals adapt themselves to a life of endless noise, high tension, lack of privacy, work with a limited set of faculties, and anonymity? Today

the number of over-stimulated and neurotic persons, the
number of misfits vocational and emotional, the number
of delinquents and criminals indicate that the present
social system is productive of wide maladjustment.
And this is true at a time of unparalleled prosperity,
when material comforts are enjoyed by a majority of
the population.

Though this analysis of the causes of social maladjustment fails to define or to illumine the subject
adequately, it may suggest the wide territory which
social work attempts to cover. Social work tends to
begin where education, industry, the state, the church,
the family have failed to provide the individual with
what he needs for adjustment to social life. It seeks
to repair the evils wrought by unemployment, low
wages, bad heredity, illness, poor environment, ignorance, immorality. Some doubt already exists as to the
possibility of social work's functioning effectively over
so wide a field. The chances of solving problems which
are clearly within the province of the state, of the
educational system, of industry, seem remote. Yet,
in the absence of a preventive and constructive program
which receives concerted backing from various social
groups, some measures must be taken to assist the
physically and mentally handicapped, the economically destitute, the aged—those helpless for whatever
reason—who appeal for social support. Members of a
number of professions assist in relieving or in rein-
stating such individuals, but the social worker usually
accepts the responsibility of assembling all necessary
aid. The characteristics of social work, the functions
undertaken, the motives by which it is actuated require
a somewhat extended discussion.

II

UNDERLYING CHARACTERISTICS AND
MOTIVES OF SOCIAL WORK

WHAT is social work? It is defined in various ways, each definition expressing as a central idea service to an individual or group, often with the benefit of the individual as the first consideration, always with the underlying purpose of promoting the welfare of the group.[1] The term "service" may mean many things as here used; it appears to cover as wide an area as human needs. Usually, "adjustment of men to their environment" or "adjustment of social relationships" is stated

[1] "Social work, then, is a form of service which attempts, on the one hand, to help the individual or family group which is out of step to attain more orderly rhythm in the march of existence, and, on the other, to remove, so far as possible, the barriers which obstruct others from achieving the best of which they are capable." Hodson, *Is Social Work Professional? A Reëxamination of the Question.* Pamphlet of the American Association of Social Workers, 1926.

"Social work includes all voluntary attempts to extend benefits in response to needs which are concerned with social relationships and which avail themselves of scientific knowledge and employ scientific methods." Cheyney, *A Definition of Social Work,* p. 26.

"By social work is meant any form of persistent and deliberate effort to improve living or working conditions in the community, or to relieve, diminish or prevent distress, whether due to weakness of character, or to pressure of external circumstances. All such efforts may be conceived as falling under the heads of charity, education or justice, and the same action may sometimes appear as one or another according to the point of view." Quoted by Flexner in "Is Social Work a Profession?" *Bulletin of the New York School of Philanthropy, 1915.*

"The subject matter of social work is the adjustment of men to their environment." Lee, Address before National Conference of Social Work, *Proceedings of the Conference, 1920.*

as the form of service undertaken, but these phrases do not succeed in making a distinction between social work and the work of the physician, the minister, the lawyer, the teacher.

Three characteristics appear to distinguish social work from other vocations. The first is that *social work takes account of the multiple needs of the individual and treats them as a unit*. In general, it may be said that the social worker accepts a wider if less intensive responsibility than other professionals, since the social worker enlists all necessary aid and provides for the treatment prescribed. A minister, for example, would refer a case outside his own field to a physician or a lawyer, and would assume that when the most pressing aspect was attended to, the matter would be successfully resolved. The social worker, on the other hand, would remain in contact with the case until it was evident whether other needs must be met, and might use half a dozen agencies before feeling that all that was requisite had been done.

A second characteristic lies in the fact that *flexibility of program is an essential of social work*. Any particular activity of the social worker may be viewed as temporary and as lacking the element of exclusiveness, but there seems no diminution in the number of services performed. New activities are taken on as former activities are absorbed into other vocations. Theoretically, one can argue as to what social work should be, the economy of having a defined province, the benefits resulting from satisfactory interrelationships and a proper division of responsibilities with medicine, public health, the social sciences, education, home economics, psychiatry, government, and other allied fields. Practically, the situation is that there is no central authority to plan for such a rational distribution of functions and certainly no machinery for supervising the working out of the plan. In the absence of mutual agreement among those attacking the problems of society as to what each shall do, there can be little hope of a clear statement of what comprises or should comprise social work.

Philanthropy probably came into existence in the face of pressing need. During centuries of development the field has broadened and changed in rather direct response to social needs. At all times the aim recognized has been the meeting of an existing situation. Whatever appears to be important for human welfare and is ignored in the program of existing social institutions has been accepted as a task for social work. There has been marked change in the concept of what is essential for human welfare and even more change in methods for effecting it. Yet, at any given moment, social work seems fairly described by saying that it supplements in whatever way needful all other work undertaken for human welfare, though confusion with other fields and indefiniteness of program may result.

A third characteristic is found to be that *social work is usually financed by society and not by the individual benefited*. This is not an absolute distinction but one of degree between social work and other fields. The public supplies free legal, medical, educational services to many persons, but, as a whole, the chief source of funds for the support of the legal and medical professions is from clients. It is exceptional for the social worker to be paid for his services by those served. There may be some contribution by the client towards payment for the treatment suggested, but there is rarely anything paid to the social worker. The situation is similar in some degree to that of education, where those who utilize public facilities may pay little or no taxes. Custodial care for dependents, defectives, and delinquents is supplied by the state, and the great body of "out-door relief," recreation, and community programs is carried on with funds furnished by private persons actuated by philanthropic motives.

The methods and objectives of social work can be understood only when the motives for its support have been analyzed. Within the complexity of these motives lies the history of philanthropy through the ages, as well as a reflection of the philosophy of the present generation, together supplying some explanation of the status of social work today. The motives of those who are making a living in social work and of those who are supporting it do not seem essentially different. Some of the professional group have adopted social work because they feel that it provides interest, remuneration, and general opportunities comparable with other vocations. Some of those supporting social work undoubtedly are seeking associations which they feel give them social standing and esteem. To a limited extent utilitarianism actuates those interested in social work as it actuates most of society. In general, however, the appeal of social work is to the disinterested; to those who, as far as they are conscious of motive, are seeking to assist others by giving either their work or their money.

At least four motives may be discerned among those interested in social work, though the individuals concerned may be more or less conscious of them. Usually one motive dominates, though several may appear in combination. The most general, the most venerable, and the most commonly recognized motive is founded upon the principles of religious, racial, and fraternal groups. Many see social work as a duty of the strong towards the weak, the fortunate towards the unfortunate. Faith in the power of Providence, acting through human agencies, to solve any existing human problem gives confidence as to results. The churches have preached good deeds as second only to faith in the duty of their members. If the idea is accepted that all human souls are of equal value in the sight of the Creator, an unanswerable argument is supplied for taking infinite pains with every individual. Hence, the church is a militant factor in attacking the sorrows and evils of the world, in bringing succor to the individual. It realizes its creed in so doing.

Where a race has achieved unity through common experiences which are of peculiar nature, a strong feeling of mutual responsibility may be developed. The Jewish people, for example, have shown at times the kind of racial solidarity which insures provision for the weak by the strong. Immigrants from foreign countries tend to form associations along nationalistic lines for the protection and advancement of the economic and social interests of their own members. Fraternal organizations, like the Loyal Order of the Moose, create a basis for mutual insurance and welfare among their members. In these various types of organizations, as in religious groups, the duty of helping the weak and of assuming responsibility for group welfare is emphasized.

Closely akin to the group which promotes social work from religious motives is a second group, actuated by *abstract ideals of democracy and social justice,* by belief that society exists for the welfare of all its members and is obligated to take definite steps to realize this end. This group, too, is made up of idealists and perfectionists, capable of sustained effort based on faith.

A third group, either small in numbers or inarticulate until recently, is professedly *practical rather than ethical in aim.* General progress, it says, must not be retarded by the lagging members of society; individual problems must be met promptly and adequately in order that society shall not suffer. Strong support is supplied by those students of society who have developed the concept of society as a biological organism, intricately formed so that an injury to a part is an injury to the whole. Following this line of thought, practical statesmanship demands a constructive program for dealing with all the diseases of society.

Much less conspicuous than any of the above-mentioned groups are a small number which constitute a fourth group, *responsive to advance in scientific knowledge and interested in exploring the possibilities of modifying human lives* to the advantage of both the individual and of society. The motive here becomes primarily scientific, and results are measured by the value and relevance of data collected, rather than by immediate benefits accruing to individuals or groups in the process of collecting these data.

Within these four groups there are many who, if asked to state their motives for being engaged in social work, would indicate that they held one or another of these attitudes towards the misfortunes of others. As far as they are conscious of their motives they will answer correctly. But the leading motive may frequently be found only in their own lives. Social work has regularly absorbed, both as contributors and as professionals, men and women whose personal misfortunes, disappointments, or colorless lives have led them to seek an outlet in the lives of others. In such cases self-interest is to be recognized as a factor. No criticism is justified on this score unless the results are bad. Yet when social organizations seek to effect an adjustment for their contributors or workers at the same time that they are carrying out a relief program, they are seldom entirely successful. Social work appears to be one of the last fields aspiring to professional status which wittingly allows its program to be shaped and carried out by persons without definite qualifications for such work. It is not probable that this practice would obtain if there were explicit recognition by the public of the responsibilities which the social welfare program assumes, or if clients paid for the services rendered them.

Those of realistic mind might deny that these motives, which have been enumerated, are chiefly responsible for the support of social work. The reasons that people subscribe to the community chest or to individual charities are three, they would say. One is that prestige in the community demands some evidence of social disinterestedness and generosity from those who can afford to give; the second is that prestige is often achieved through generous gifts by those seeking social position; and the third is that there is a genuine emotional response to those in distress, which is characteristic of humanity.

It is admitted that these three reasons are immediate and effective in bringing in subscriptions. The rational motives form, however, the underlying explanation of why support of social work assures community prestige, and also why individuals feel a double satisfaction in yielding to their sympathetic impulses towards the poor. The intelligent layman appreciates the existence of a rational basis for asking his support as a member of society, though his immediate reactions to the appeal for a subscription may be entirely personal.

There may seem to be no persistent reason why the various motives noted should produce confusion in the methods and objectives of social work. The religious motive and the abstract ethical motive arrive at about the same position; emphasis upon the practical advantage to society of taking care of all its members may lead to a program exactly similar to that based upon either of the first mentioned motives. There is, furthermore, a connecting link between the common-sense motive and the scientific, in that the actual workings of society must be observed and used as the basis of both programs. Certainly, the disparity in motives seems no wider than that found in all professions from the ministry to government, and in certain of these a definite and satisfactory status has been achieved. Why, then, are diverse motives held responsible for the weaknesses of the social work program?

It would be more accurate to say that diverse motives in attacking the vast province of social maladjustments produce confusion because there is no common program. Possibly a program may be drawn which would make profitable use of groups having varied interests and motivation, but recognition of common purposes must, of necessity, determine the program. Two lawyers might give widely different reasons for practicing law; yet there should not be great difficulty in securing from them a statement as to the scope and function of the law. But two social workers representing opposite interests, on the one hand, of reform for the glory of religion, and on the other, of research into human affairs for the enrichment of science, would present extremes in outlook upon social work which might prevent apperception of common interests. The combination of diverse motives and an undefined field of activity brings forth uncertain methods and objectives as its fruits.

The religious motive and the abstract ethical motive are perhaps less accented today than those motives which are attributed to common sense and interest in scientific progress, but it may be safely asserted that the main support for social work still comes from those who are influenced by the first two motives. There is little of emotional appeal in the common-sense motive, and, besides, there is not convincing proof of the identical interests of the individual and of the group. An ability to view life with detachment and with long perspective is necessary to the common-sense point of view. Enthusiasm for any particular program is not likely to flourish when there is emphasis upon viewing all problems in the large. The scientific approach has the emotional appeal which the common-sense motive lacks, but there are few persons impelled by it to interest themselves in social work. Those who see social work as a promising field for experiment are apt to take little thought of its general problems. Little of what they achieve—to date, their direct contributions to practical problems are inconsiderable—permeates to the larger groups approaching social work from other angles.

Lack of direct contributions from the scientific group may be due to interference from other groups in the carrying out of satisfactory experiments. Those who have ethical or religious aims may have rather fixed ideas both as to what is desirable to achieve and as to methods of achievement. Until science is more sure of itself in dealing with human lives, there will be a reluctance among non-scientific groups to collaborate in experiment. This is natural enough but it virtually precludes science from moving forward rapidly. In matters of social welfare there is reflected the general attitude towards scientific method—interest amounting to fascination, respect, and outward acceptance, but lethargy and a deep-seated aversion to concrete applications. There is already a great lag between knowledge as to social problems and practical application.[2]

The difficulty that is met in producing clear-cut

[2] "Knowledge far outruns practice. There is no longer doubt that delinquency could be checked, practically eliminated from the normal population, if a sufficient number of social workers would dedicate their lives to application of scientific knowledge of behavior we now possess." Van Waters, *Youth in Conflict*, p. 243.

results from any kind of social welfare program puts on the defensive any group which claims superiority for one method over another. Diverse motives are not primarily to blame for the lack of definite objectives and unity in welfare programs. More important is the uncertainty of long-run results from any kind of social enterprise. Few are so rash as to claim ability to measure social change in terms of definite progress. Change and progress are both relative terms, permitting broad interpretation. Neither is easily brought about by a welfare program. In a given social situation so many factors enter in, and control over most of them is so slight, that results can very seldom be brought about or measured according to preconceived plan. When no type of social work can claim very positive results, the public is handicapped in electing those to be financed.

Reference to those interested in social work has included directors and trustees of social organizations, contributors and promoters, as well as those having social work as a vocation. The general public, in fact, determines the social welfare program. The medical, the legal, the engineering professions shape their policies without consultation with non-professionals. It is true that educators must carry city councils and state legislatures along when they propose any increases in expenditures for which public funds must be obtained, and they have boards of control with whom they must fight out questions of policy. They have, nevertheless, an established claim to public moneys and are becoming increasingly loath to accept private funds conditioned by personal points of view.

The social work of private agencies, like the church, depends largely upon voluntary gifts from individuals for its support. Even today the church has a more definite claim for support than has social work, since it has a creed, canons, and the Scriptures making explicit the duty of its members. In social work there is uncertainty as to the motive to be stressed when urging support. The older generation of social workers is able to voice an "idealistic" philosophy without self-consciousness and with sincere conviction in the possibilities of achievement. The younger generation, schooled in a more sceptical and sophisticated period, "unsettled" in its religious convictions by some knowledge of science, and distressed by the need of unqualified endorsement of any program upon the basis of anticipated results, wavers in the task of arousing the public emotionally to the support of social work.[3] These young people have neither sufficient faith in their ideals nor satisfactory proof of practical results upon which to base an impassioned appeal.

At the same time that the social worker hesitates to assert the infallibility of his program, the public is

[3] "Social work, if the conference at Cleveland is a fair cross section of it, has lost its emotional authority. It hesitates to proclaim itself now (except for campaign purposes) as pure altruism. It has lost its direct connection with the Church. It has not yet attained the coherence and solidarity of a profession with its own sufficient traditions. It is not sure of its relation to the emotional storehouses of the class struggle or of experimental democracy. It has hardly assimilated its own scientific premises with sufficient thoroughness to be greatly moved by scientific enthusiasm. It has become too practical to be passionate. But the old emotional impulses linger. The older social workers are troubled by their evident weakening. The younger ones are too busy to reason why. There is an unstable spiritual equilibrium." Smith, "Behemoth Walks Again," *The Survey*, LVI (June 15, 1926), 360.

becoming deaf to arguments which are not of compelling nature. Advertising methods have so influenced habits of thought that overstatement seems necessary to stir any response. A natural reaction may in the future enlist the public's confidence and interest where there is conservative appraisal or understatement. Just now, social organizations seem to be using the publicity methods prevalent and are devoting much of the skill at their command towards advertising their work. The justification lies in the fact that results are achieved. Still, criticism may be made of the emphasis of much publicity upon raising money, rather than upon informing the public of the nature of the work. One hears the statement that social organizations have no money for educational work with the public. It is also said that much of the welfare work that should be done has to be left undone because the public is unaware of its value and does not give financial support. Satisfactory financing of social work can be achieved only when those who support it have an understanding of what social work is trying to do, why it has set certain goals, how it is succeeding in its tasks. The public must be convinced that methods and objectives in social work have been harmonized, though support may be elicited by appealing to various motives. If a program capable of inspiring enthusiasm and confidence were drawn, more adequate financing might be assured. Difficult as the job is, it appears, therefore, that the public must be educated, its motives subjected to self-examination, its impulses unified and directed towards sound objectives, before a successful program in social welfare work can be put into effect. The alternative that social work is to be carried on by a professional group, which will be self-sufficient financially and capable of achieving its objectives without public backing, seems unlikely of realization.

III

SOURCES OF FINANCIAL SUPPORT
FOR SOCIAL WORK

SOCIAL work has been shown to be a product of the existing social organization. The range of human lives within which social work is recognized as an active factor is quite definitely determined by economic status. Social work today is an outgrowth of the charity of the past. The methods and objectives of social work may be very different from the philanthropy of twenty-five years ago, but its clients still come largely from those who have little or no economic margin.[1] Ignorance and ill health, the incidence of industrial progress, number their victims largely in the lower economic classes. Those who live at the margin have no material or intellectual reserves upon which to draw when a crisis arises. The social worker is called in when an accident, unemployment, illness, or non-social behavior creates a problem. Sometimes, it is true, there is no question of financial assistance, and the social worker advises and summons the agents needed for adjustment. If knowledge of community resources were general, many calls upon social organizations would be eliminated.

The social worker seems to play little part in the

[1] The recreational programs of the Y. M. C. A., the Y. W. C. A., the Boy Scouts, the Girl Scouts, Community Houses, etc., draw from various economic classes.

lives of those well situated economically. When there are sufficient funds, specialists are called directly, and the client himself assumes the responsibility of directing the forces of adjustment. Individualism asserts itself and usually nothing short of economic necessity will persuade those in distress to accept free service. There is mounting evidence that such independence often handicaps the individual, since he might benefit by many offerings of the community to which he is entitled. Some are beginning to recognize that the best medical advice is to be secured at clinics, and that certain privileges are offered by the state to its citizens which cannot be bought elsewhere.

The self-maintaining individual is not likely even in the future to identify all of his interests with those of the group and to allow his life to be organized for him. As a rule, the social worker has little opportunity to work with intelligent people of means. He is not, perhaps, in as strong a position to offer valuable advice as when dealing with those unaware of what the community affords or unable financially to secure help. There is little to show that the social worker is achieving status as a new kind of specialist to whom all classes will resort for advice upon questions relating to social relationships and adjustments. The social worker is called *instead* of the lawyer, the doctor, the engineer, or some other kind of specialist, by those whose limited social knowledge or financial resources necessitate their having a counselor. The majority of those supporting social work would be surprised to think of themselves as possible recipients of such help except in case of economic destitution.

If the point of view is accepted that social work exists chiefly for the benefit of the "disadvantaged" economically,[2] it is plain how closely social work is bound up with a system producing defined economic classes. This interpretation of social work may be in the minds of those who complain that it is a prop to the present economic system. Also, much of that which determines the personnel, methods, and scope of social work is explained.

Since social work is financed by those who do not usually expect to benefit directly by it, the principle of altruism is all-pervasive. Those who enter social work as a vocation reflect the various attitudes mentioned in the first chapter. Few would say outright that their controlling idea was to earn a livelihood in a congenial profession. Over and over again old social workers reiterate that desire to serve humanity must be the leading motive, else discontent will soon appear. It is true that social work offers little to those eager for material reward. There is no promise that salaries will be in proportion to value of services; salaries are based much more nearly on cost of living.[3]

The social evaluation of social work may be said to be the amount society subscribes for maintaining it.[4] The situation is unusual in that the service is usually appraised by those who do not experience it—perhaps an erroneous method of determining value. Since those who supply the funds for social work do not expect any material benefit for themselves, they are inclined

[2] Or to prevent others from becoming so.
[3] Russell Sage Study, 1925. (Unpublished), see p. 105n.
[4] In a way the contributing public pays for the service of being relieved of individual responsibility.

to project their own point of view upon those professionally engaged in it. That is, they assume that adequate personnel can be secured for salaries just sufficient to insure decent living. Social workers have a disinterested attitude towards material reward thrust upon them and are expected to assist in making the salary levy upon welfare funds as small as possible. Furthermore, social workers are often in the position of raising budgets—in which their own salaries are included—for welfare activities. They have the responsibility of showing the public that a pressing situation, calling for financial aid, exists. In presenting the situation to others, it is difficult to emphasize their own salary claims. As a result, social workers frequently appear to accept the point of view that they should offer their services for as small an economic return as is compatible with common sense. Their claim for public confidence seems dependent upon the adoption of such an attitude; yet it is doubtful whether society does not underestimate social workers for the very reason that they are not remunerated according to a businesslike appraisal of their services. The tendency is deep-seated to judge a man by the salary he commands.

Once the idea is implanted that as small an allocation as possible should be made for salaries, a serious handicap to social work is threatened. For the peculiarity of social work—that those who pay for it do not experience it—means that the effectiveness of those employed is difficult to check upon. Hence insistence upon a low overhead cost in social work may interfere with a successful and constructive program, if low-salaried employees are considered, ipso facto, satisfactory, and if there is little opportunity among those passing judgment to test the quality of the work being done.

A sounder basis for fixing salaries would be to pay the amount necessary to obtain effective employees. Salary adjustments must, however, wait upon the establishment of standards as to what constitutes effective work. These standards social workers themselves must demonstrate.

Absence of such checks as the balance sheet and cost accounting afford to business appears to explain to some extent the lack of standards for measuring the cost and value of the services of the social worker. A serious possibility arises that work may be inefficient, when those supplying the funds are not able to judge the quality of service rendered, and when those receiving are not expected to criticize services for which they pay nothing.[5] Persons of no particular skill or training are permitted to enter this field as a vocation, because those who support social work have reached no agreement as to the purpose for which social work is carried on and, accordingly, have set no definite qualifications for social workers. If the statements of leading social workers are accepted as to the important responsibilities assumed, the educational background and experience called for, it is apparent that large numbers of social workers are not qualified for what they are doing.

An unbusinesslike attitude towards social work is

[5] "Our social workers and our uplift organizations do not know what results they are getting, and by what methods they are getting them in the rigorous sense in which a well-managed business corporation knows what it is getting out of its personnel, its machines, and its methods." Giddings, *The Scientific Study of Human Society*, p. 41.

reflected in the operation of some private social organizations. Many of the trustees and directors of charities believe that the heart and not the head should be consulted in making a program for social work. There is positive satisfaction in knowing that so many tons of coal were delivered, so many children sent to summer camps, so many patients given treatment at a clinic. In a field where the amelioration of human ills is the goal, it is natural that tangible results should be welcomed. If there is too great insistence upon getting results which can be measured, the social worker may be limited, however, to a narrow field of social welfare.

Private social agencies sometimes undertake activities without a thorough examination of general social needs. Where the public bears the expense of certain activities, there is at least a rough attempt to determine how and by what group these enterprises may be most economically carried on. When charitable impulses supply the funds and direct the policies, there is a tendency to undertake any kind of work which comes to hand, with no particular thought given as to whether there is needless duplication of effort and overlapping with other fields. For example, in some city orphan asylums maintained by religious bodies the children go to school on the premises, though public schools with far better equipment and opportunities for a more normal social life may be within a stone's throw. And when the activity, sound or unsound, has been determined upon, there is no guarantee that ordinary precautions will be taken to run it along economical and efficient lines. In office organization, purchasing, and disbursement of funds, accredited business practices are often ignored.

Changes are apt to take place in the management of social welfare organizations. The possibility that social work may beome a self-sufficing vocation, offering services for which full payment is made by the client, is dismissed as remote. To those who are able to pay for the services they need, other professionals than social workers appear to be preferred. There is much evidence to support the view, however, that welfare work will be organized and administered in a more businesslike way than in the past. The growth of the community chest movement has greatly modified practices within the past seven or eight years. Where there is a chest, a uniform system of accounting usually prevails among the constituent agencies; a centralized purchasing department, publicity and research divisions are in effect. Furthermore, a chest or federation of agencies leads to careful analysis and evaluation of services based upon general community interests. The tendency is to curb individualistic philanthropy and to work towards an adequate social program rather than to emphasize a particular type of activity. With the coming of the chest there is usually a clearer enunciation of the philosophy of social work; the social responsibility of the individual citizen and the interrelationships of society are made explicit.

The community chest has developed rapidly in the United States and appears to have been an effective means of organizing the accelerated interest in community welfare which was an outgrowth of the World War. A large increase in the amount of money available for private social agencies has come within the past decade. The National Bureau of Economic Research has published the results of the study of a test city, New Haven, which shows the trend in receipts of social agencies during the period 1900 to 1925. In New Haven, which has had a well-managed community chest since 1921 and has a satisfactory accounting system among member agencies, ninety social organizations reporting in 1925 received more than ten times as many dollars as did the forty-one for which information covering the year 1900 was secured. The ninety-nine religious organizations included were given three times as much money in 1923, their most prosperous year, as the seventy-nine organizations then existing received in 1900. In the case of both social and religious organizations the rate of growth in receipts has been more rapid since 1914 than before. The figures have not been corrected to allow for changes in the purchasing power of the dollar, but there has been an absolute increase.

Increase in the number of both religious and social organizations during the quarter-century is worthy of note; also, the fact that the proportional rate of growth of contributions to social agencies has been materially greater than that to religious organizations. While the increase in income of religious organizations showed a smooth upward trend from 1904 to 1923, there has been a moderate decline since 1923. The rate of increase in income of social agencies has diminished since 1920 and the trend appears to be toward a more or less stationary amount.[6]

Compilations of data by the Association of Community Chests and Councils verify the New Haven

[6] National Bureau of Economic Research, *News Bulletin* No. 24 (March 30, 1927).

data as to the diminishing rate of increase in amounts raised by chests. While together sixty-eight community chests, which have been in operation five years, raised 19.3 per cent more for 1927 than they did for 1923, they raised only 1.3 per cent more for 1927 than they did for 1926. The per cent of increase for 1924 over 1923 was 7.6 per cent. These data are variously interpreted by those interested in the financing of social work. Many have begun to talk of the "saturation point in giving" and believe that larger amounts for welfare work can be obtained only through economies in operation or by securing tax funds. Others maintain that the chests have overworked the idea of "business efficiency" both in appeals and in attempts to apply methods of the business world to welfare activities. They claim that the chests will find that returns are constant or diminishing, unless they place their emphasis upon the social and spiritual needs of the community. When the public recognizes authentic social need, there is held to be no limit to giving.[7]

Another group of critics question the ultimate success of the community-chest movement because they see in it a negation of the natural desire of the charitable to support an individual or a cause which has a direct, emotional appeal. In emphasizing community needs there may be little opportunity to give the citizens a close-up view of particular social organizations. The personal contact between the giver and the recipient

[7] Holbrook, *The Saturation Point in Giving.*

This point of view is supported by certain current events: The new Medical Center of Columbia University is to cost $25,000,000; this year the *New York Times* raised about $180,000 in its appeal to the public for "The Hundred Neediest Cases" at Christmas time.

may be lost and with it the spark which makes charity something more than a duty. If the economy, the efficiency, and the thoroughness of the community-chest method are stressed at the expense of the human interest side of welfare work, support may in time come grudgingly, or only from a desire for social approbation and advancement. This is not only a loss to the treasury of possible funds but also a loss to the general community of a unifying and unselfish interest.

Community chests are, however, inclined towards self analysis and are carrying on a number of studies designed to shape future policy. A very valuable piece of work has been completed showing the social resources of nineteen large community-chest cities in the United States. Comparative costs of different services are given in detail.[8] In time, standards may thus be developed as to what are the minimum services a city must offer, what combination of social organizations shows best results, what is the necessary cost of such welfare work. With such data in hand the education of the public and the raising of funds should be greatly simplified.

While the chest movement does not cover all cities nor even some of the most important ones—neither New York nor Chicago has a chest—it is the most characteristic method of financing private social work in American cities. The Association of Community Chests and Councils estimates that over sixty million dollars is raised each year by three hundred community

[8] Clapp, *Study of Volume and Cost of Social Work, 1924: Tabulation of Income for Nineteen Cities.* Pamphlet of American Assn. for Community Organization (May 25, 1926).

chests in cities which receive an additional ninety million dollars from earnings, interest on endowment, and tax appropriations.[9] While community chests are criticized both as to the theories upon which they are founded and as to the practices which they have initiated, there seems a wide consensus of opinion that they will persist. Though the record does not show unqualified success, it is still a record of steady progress.

The chest movement does not cover all private welfare organizations nor those maintained exclusively on tax funds. Some religious organizations and some strongly individualistic private agencies remain outside. The effect of the chest is probably felt none the less. When satisfactory methods of financial accounting and of evaluating and coördinating services are developed for chest members, such methods tend to be adopted by publicly maintained organizations. One of the most important functions of the privately supported agency is to set standards for tax-supported welfare activities. The public is educated to demand proper management of its institutions when an example is given of possible achievement. Absence of standards has undoubtedly had much to do with society's obtuseness to the question of proper care of its wards. The treatment of delinquents and criminals may lag behind treatment of other non-social individuals because the state has so jealously guarded its control of this group, while it has shared with private organizations the care of other defectives and dependents. The responsibility of protecting society from its dangerous members has often seemed greater than any responsibility felt for

[9] *News about Community Chests,* May 1, 1927.

the reinstatement of those members. Experiment in treating criminals has been limited, since the state tends to be more conservative and less flexible than private organizations in its methods.

Any attempt to distinguish sharply between privately controlled and tax-supported welfare activities is apt to be unsuccessful, since there is no definite line of demarcation between them. It may be possible to indicate which activities are usually in the hands of private and which in the hands of public organizations, the relative amount of welfare work on tax funds as compared to that supported privately, but there will be no data of conclusive nature. The trend may be noted, but no absolute statement can be made as to the territory proper to each type of activity.

As to activities usually supported on public funds, the appropriations made by New York State, County, and City, will furnish some light. New York State maintains institutions for the insane, the feeble-minded, the epileptic, the blind, the deaf, the dumb, the crippled, the tubercular, the physically ill, the destitute, the aged, the delinquent, and the criminal. There are privately maintained institutions for each of these groups except the criminal, but the State bears the greater part of the burden of institutional care. Institutions for child-caring and for the aged are more often privately than publicly supported.

In addition to providing institutions, the State renders welfare service of various kinds. Through Mothers' Aid a large number of children are maintained by the State in their own homes. The Board of Child Welfare and the State Board of Charities care

for many dependent children and families through
outdoor relief. The State maintains a Health Department which carries on numerous activities through
such divisions as Public Health Nursing, Maternity,
Infancy, and Child Hygiene, Public Health Education,
County Health Projects. The Department of Mental
Hygiene also has several divisions including one for
prevention of mental disease. The State maintains
an extensive playground and state park system. The
State has a fairly comprehensive system of compensation insurance for industrial accidents and disease.
Appropriations are made for vocational guidance, State
employment offices, industrial and immigrant education. All these welfare activities of the State are
supplemented by privately maintained activities.

The relative amounts of tax and private funds supporting welfare work are not easily discovered. It is
simple enough to learn how much a community chest
of a certain city distributes among its constituent
members within a year. But many private organizations
carrying on welfare work are not members of the chests.
The individual amounts appropriated for social welfare by the city, the county, and the state may be
found by careful study of the records of legislative
bodies. No general reports, showing such appropriations classified and totaled, are available. It is practically impossible to learn from any official or bureau
what lump sums are devoted to this purpose. Not only
is the general public unaware of what is expended for
social welfare, but none of its representatives appears
to have ascertained the total amount.

In the absence of exact data only general statements as to trends and ratios of expenditures can be made. Lack of research in the field of income and expenditure necessitates the use of incomplete and inconclusive data. If undue emphasis appears to be placed upon a few studies, the explanation lies in the fact that no more representative data are available.

The Association of Community Chests and Councils together with the Welfare Federation of Cleveland during 1924 conducted a coöperative experiment in social welfare census-taking in American chest cities.[10] The study included under the heading "Welfare Activities" all services of the types usually financed by a community fund, together with parallel government activities. The chief types of agencies were those concerned with dependency, delinquency, health, character building through group work, coördination, and planning. The inclusion of hospitals and the exclusion of institutions for the insane, the feeble-minded and epileptic, all reformatories and prisons, all churches, all propagandist agencies, all libraries, parks, and court officials should be noted. Some differences in practice between cities, and, therefore, differences in meaning of classifications, were inevitable. Bearing these limitations in mind, the general conclusions still have value. In 1924 the grand total income for welfare work in these nineteen cities was $112,780,524. Of this amount 43 per cent ($47,872,544) was earned by the welfare agencies; 57 per cent ($64,907,980) was unearned income derived from three sources: *Contributions*, $25,339,150; *Endowment*, $4,593,128; *Taxes*, $34,975,702. Public

[10] Clapp, *op. cit.*

revenue or taxes constituted 31 per cent, while contributions and endowment together amounted to only 26 per cent of the grand total income. In three cities tax revenues amounted to more than earnings.

The distribution of income by allotments to various services are of interest:

Health.........................$	54,730,657
Dependency.....................	28,041,286
Character building...............	25,169,623
Delinquency....................	2,951,282
Coördination...................	1,701,377
Miscellaneous...................	186,299

$ 112,780,524 [11]

Another unpublished study by Richard K. Conant, Massachusetts State Commissioner of Public Welfare, gives certain data upon public welfare expenditures during 1924 by cities in the United States with over 500,000 population. Percentages of total income of these cities distributed for classfied welfare activities are as follows:

Per cent   1924   *Service*
  6.9 of all city expenses charged to Charities
  3.3 of all city expenses charged to Recreation
10.5 of all city expenses charged to Health and Sanitation
20.0 of all city expenses charged to Protection of Person
 ——   and Property
40.7 total city expenses charged to Welfare Activities

As to what the terms "charities," "recreation," etc. connote, each city has been a law to itself, according to

[11] Clapp, *ibid.*

Mr. Conant. The value of the data lies in indicating the relative expense of different services to the city.

Several studies of individual cities have been made. The public and private expenditures for welfare in New York City in 1923 were analyzed by the Bureau of Advice and Information of the Charity Organization Society with the idea of furnishing some important data as to the cost of social work to the contributing public, and also with the idea of furthering the better coördination of welfare activities. Figures from 474 private agencies and seven public departments were compiled. The sum of $70,050,374 was found to have been expended by these organizations during the fiscal year 1923. Of this amount approximately 37 per cent was raised by taxation. As there are nearly 2,000 organizations listed in the Directory of Social Agencies of Greater New York, it is apparent that many were not included in this study.[12] National agencies, those working in the foreign field, state-wide agencies, fraternal groups, foundations, churches, educational and cultural agencies were omitted. Furthermore, the appropriations of the city for protection, health, education, recreation, and institutional care of dependents were only included in part. The City Budget for 1923 showed the following items:

[12] A later estimate (1927) made by the Research Committee of the Welfare Council of New York City gives $100,000,000 as the approximate amount expended annually by New York organizations. Special bulletin of the Welfare Council of New York City. "Is Welfare Work Worth its Cost?" Hodson (December, 1927).

Unfortunate and Dependents
    Hospitals, Charitable Institutions, Child
      Welfare, etc........................$ 23,618,687.48

Protection
    Conservation of Public Health, Health
      Department, Street Cleaning, Tene-
      ment House Department, etc.........   29,976,390.33

Education and Recreation
    Schools, Colleges, Libraries, Museums,
      Playgrounds, etc...................   88,780,473.52

           City Appropriations............$ 142,375,551.33

The items from city appropriations, included in the total of $70,050,324 for both private and public agencies as given in the 1923 study, are:

Department of Public Welfare...........$	6,767,816.56
Board of Child Welfare.................	4,275,013.20
Department of Health..................	4,732,584.13
Bellevue and allied hospitals............	2,542,248.48
Parole Commission.....................	104,753.64
Children's Court.......................	336,524.64
Board of Education (Special activities)....	393,005.60
Commitment of Insane.................	6,400.00
$	19,158,346.25

The activities covered in the second list are held to be more or less comparable with those of the private agencies included in the study. In addition to the welfare activities which the city itself maintains on tax funds, the city contributed nearly seven millions to the welfare activities of private organizations. This constituted 15 per cent of the total income of the 352 private agencies for which complete data were secured. Earnings constituted 45 per cent of the income of the private agencies, while donations (26 per cent) and interest on investments (11 per cent) together supplied 35 per cent of income.[13]

As in other studies mentioned, the inclusion of hospitals among welfare activities greatly augments the totals both of disbursements and of earnings. The private agencies of New York during 1923 expended nearly twenty-three millions (45 per cent of their income) upon hospitals. The earnings from hospitals amounted to 63 per cent of their expenses. The exclusion from the study of a number of activities—such as parks and playgrounds—is not, on the face, self-explanatory. If the above total of $70,050,324 were augmented by the addition of the amounts expended for activities of quasi-welfare character, the grand total would be very large indeed. The city spent over eight million dollars (out of the $19,158,346 charged to welfare activities) upon hospitals.[14]

It would be interesting to compare the amounts spent upon public welfare by the state, county, and municipality respectively. A few states, like Massachusetts, may be able to supply these data. A great deal of work would be necessary to secure them for New York. The practice of allowing each department to issue a separate report at no specified date means that no satisfactory estimate of total appropriations for the current year can be made. The sums derived from private sources for welfare work throughout the State

[13] King and Frear, "The Finances of New York's Social Work," *Better Times*, June 1, 1925, pp. 21-29.   [14] *Ibid.* pp. 22, 26.

are not ascertainable. The statement is found in various reports that approximately $250,000,000 is annually spent in the State for charity, benevolence, relief, etc. What activities are included and how accurate the estimate is, cannot be said.

An approximate estimate of New York State appropriations during 1926-1927 for various welfare activities (including institutions, state prisons, and parks, hospitals, playgrounds, reformatories) is about $130,000,000. Of this amount, sixty-two million is distributed by the Board of Child Welfare, thirty-four million by the State Board of Charities, and over seventeen million for State institutions.[15]

Little may be concluded from statistical data except that the total amounts expended for welfare activities are large, are increasing, and are derived in great part from tax funds. It is not possible to present conclusive proof that the state is undertaking an increasing portion of the burden of public welfare, since comparable figures of public and private expenditures are available neither for the past nor for the present. It can be shown that certain activities once supported as private philanthropies have come to be regarded as permanent public activities. In Europe, unemployment doles, social insurance of various kinds, workmen's compensation have long been sponsored by the government. In the United States, as elsewhere, much of the hitherto privately financed social work program—such as mothers' pensions, maternity benefits, hospital care, playgrounds—has recently become part of a public educational or health program supported out of

[15] Compilations from reports of various state departments, 1926-27.

taxes.[16] Within twenty-five years many extensions and additions have been made in public service. Public provision for institutional care of the defective and the ill has become more adequate and private funds have been partially withdrawn from this work to be applied elsewhere. Public health nursing was to great extent dependent upon private funds when initiated and, until recently, was chiefly financed in rural regions by the American Red Cross. Now, the county, the state, and the municipality are supplying this service. Throughout the health field the increase in public support is noticeable.

There was formerly less flexibility in the public welfare program than at present. Dependent children were placed in institutions; out-door relief was given in the form of groceries, coal, rent, and was limited by a fixed maximum. Following the leadership set by private agencies, the dependent child is now supported by the state in the way which best conserves the individual interest, whether this means placement in an institution or in a foster home, or maintenance in his own home. The nation-wide adoption of mothers' pension laws has meant the acceptance of a new philosophy of human welfare by the state—prevention rather than relief of destitution recognized as a goal. The same principle is at work when the state establishes an employment service, state compensation insurance, a division of public health education, a comprehensive plan for out-door recreation. In the majority of these services the state is following where private welfare has blazed the trail. When the effectiveness of a certain

[16] Cheyney, *Op. cit.*, p. 14.

method of treatment has been demonstrated, and when evidence has been brought that the situation in which that method functions is a persistent one, the state may appropriately assume the task of providing that service.

When the state should assume a responsibility which involves financial support is not always crystal-clear. The long-time results of welfare activities are difficult to measure; they may not take concrete form. Can it be definitely established, for instance, that allowing a mother a pension for each minor child, when the father is dead or disabled, is a better method of handling than placement in institutions? It is impossible to find two exactly analagous situations to try out the two methods. Yet, the effects of institutional life upon small children have furnished an incentive to try out a new method. Also, the state was apparently influenced by the experience of private agencies, consciously dedicated to the preservation of the home, which endorse mothers' pensions. Furthermore, the social worker's recommendation of mothers' aid had good backing from the everyday experience and informal observations of the general public itself. Change can more readily be brought about when the reasons for it are demonstrable, or when they accord with common-sense judgment.

The foregoing discussion suggests that no definite province can be said to belong to public welfare as distinguished from private welfare activities. The same activities are carried on simultaneously by both public and private organizations in state, county, and municipality. That overlapping should result between the various public services, as well as between public and private services, is natural enough. The line of demarcation between the responsibilities of the various governmental units is faintly drawn. Not only is this true where welfare activities are concerned, but in other activities of public concern, such as education, health, sanitation, road building, housing, transportation, etc. The State furnishes factory inspection for New York City but the city supplies inspection for enforcing the Tenement House Law. The federal government seeks to enforce prohibition in New York City in the absence of sufficient state or local backing for the national law. The city appropriates the major part of the public school budget but receives a pro rata appropriation from state funds. State, county, and city support hospitals and public health programs.

No philosophy has been adhered to in determining public welfare activities. Tradition and recognition of an immediate problem appear to determine what the state or the county or the city is willing to undertake. In different sections of the country widely diverse points of view exist as to the proper sphere of governmental activities. In Georgia, the State had a law upon its statutes until 1910 that no tax funds could be used for high school education. Plainly the attitude towards public high school education prevailing throughout the United States was slow in penetrating to Georgia. The far western states have created state departments and boards which seem socialistic to other states. State industrial commissions, compensation insurance funds, immigration and housing commissions are recent innovations and not yet widespread.

The functions undertaken by city bodies are even more diverse than those of states. Experimental laboratories, health clinics, day nurseries, school nurses and dentists, municipal bands, summer camps, public baths, and many other welfare activities are carried on city tax funds which were formerly paid for by the individual or supplied by private philanthropy. There is clearly no activity which can be said to be peculiar to private agencies and without parallel in a publicly supported agency.

Future developments in operating methods and in financing of welfare work will probably be in line with the trends now evident. Through community chests, welfare federations, state, county, and city councils of social agencies the program of private organizations will be unified; businesslike methods of estimating costs and results will be extended; the sphere in which privately supported social activities are most effective will be determined. At the same time, public administrators will be considering welfare problems from the standpoint of governmental responsibility. Already there are indications that some are awake to the need of study as to what kind of welfare activities should be publicly financed and administered.[17] A survey of welfare work carried on by states, counties, and cities should give information upon a number of subjects: the legislation under which welfare activities are carried on, the amount of public appropriations, the

[17] In July 1927 the National Institute of Public Administration, in New York City, invited fifteen persons active in the field of public welfare to discuss just this question.

organization of welfare boards and departments, the costs of the various services, the success of present methods. Out of such knowledge there should be formulated a clarifying philosophy. With an understanding of why the public has certain responsibilities towards the unfortunate and ill-adjusted, there should also come a greater concern for meeting such responsibilities. A comprehensive program of social control in which education, health improvement, industrial progress, government, and social amelioration would each have a place might be the result of a quickened sense of public responsibility.

It appears most probable that social work will follow in the way of education, becoming tax-supported to greater and greater extent. Backing for such a statement is found in developments of the past twenty years in welfare activities and from the analogy between social work and education. Tax support of social work which is of proved value and essential to the public interest appears both proper and expedient in a democracy. There may always be the important rôle of pioneer, experimenter, and challenger, which privately supported social activities will continue to fill; the responsibilities of public activities will be, of necessity, more numerous and of more general scope.

Tax support of social work should mean that the individual receiving service would feel himself in a position to demand satisfactory attention. It should further mean that in time personnel would be selected upon qualifications for a definite piece of work with compensation adjusted to the value of the service. In saying this is what "should" result, much is being assumed as to future improvement in publicly administered activities. Certainly there is little proof at present of superior efficiency in publicly controlled enterprises—the political spoils system, party affiliations, difficulty in fixing responsibility are factors preventing progress in government management. Admitting all these arguments against extensions of government control, ultimate recognition of social responsibility for meeting evils inherent in the existing social system seems inevitable.

Furthermore, there is little hope of an adequate program of social control except through the state. The interrelationships of society are so complex that the biological concept of an organism which suffers in all its parts from an injury to one part appears quite convincing. Whereas the terms "neighborhood" and "community life" formerly had definite meaning, the areas indicated today are more extensive and of necessity vague. There is a falling off in sense of responsibility towards those immediately at hand—the anonymity of the city means that those who live in the same house or in the same block may not know each other by sight. So, it is hard to build up a group feeling which will insure a sense of civic duty and responsibility. Those who go from the city into the country are amazed to find how strong neighborhood ties are and how naturally community burdens are assumed by the stronger members. There may be ways of re-creating small community interests in the city, but it appears more likely that there will have to be a program of social welfare sponsored by the whole city. The community chest movement in many large cities is a recognition of the principle that the city's social interests are unified. The next step would seem to be to carry community programs on tax funds rather than by private subscriptions. The advantages of chest organization have been proved, but there is indication of an increasing difficulty in arousing the old philanthropic impulse to which chests must appeal. Many individuals are interested in only a single type of social work; their imagination cannot easily be fired with a program of general social reconstruction. The insurance of obligatory support through taxation may be a necessary measure.

Social work is found to have a number of economic implications: the prevailing profit economy and its characteristic methods produce many of the evils which necessitate remedial and preventive work; social progress, with its absorption in power over material resources, creates complex problems of human maladjustments; individualism, characteristic of a profit economy, places social work upon a philanthropic basis and still believes that "enlightened self interest" furnishes a sound basis for the social activities of the normal and self-sufficient. Social work, supported to considerable extent by private funds, suffers from the variety of motives which influence charitably inclined individuals. The regulating factors of demand and supply have little effect in determining the amount of social work which the community undertakes, since those who pay for social work seldom use what it provides. The personnel administering the social work program is not judged by business standards and is not paid according to the value of services rendered. There is a distinct limiting of social work to an economic class unable to pay for the services of specialists in the professions. No economic standards are applied to the methods used in social work and no results are produced which can be so measured.

Within the existing situation there is little to indicate that social work can emancipate itself from control by the general public; no economic basis for a self-supporting profession is found to exist. Difficulties in the way of making social work conform to sound economic principles—i.e., of determining what its cost should be in relation to the values created and of meeting costs through services rendered—seem much the same as the difficulties which prevent social work's achieving a definite and satisfactory status as an occupation. The situation cannot be altered markedly unless those who are the objects of social welfare work show themselves able and willing to pay for it, or unless the public identifies the general interest with the individual interest and supports all welfare work through taxation. The likelihood of the individual's being able to pay for all the services he needs is remote. Social services have been established because individuals get into positions from which they are helpless to extricate themselves. Lack of funds to meet an emergency often is the immediate incentive for seeking help. This state of affairs will probably continue and either public or private funds must continue to supply relief. In either case, social work will not be self-supporting.

IV

OBJECTIVES OF SOCIAL WORK

THE recognized ills of society are numerous and persistent. Social welfare work has grown to be an accepted part of the social system, since individuals and groups continue to look for help outside themselves in adjusting to existing situations. Large numbers of the population live under circumstances which render physical or mental well-being, the enjoyment and understanding of life, impossible. Ignorance, inferior mental or physical condition, and the unfortunate incidence of social progress appear to cause the majority of individual maladjustments. For the next half-century there will probably be an extension in remedial work for the care of defectives, delinquents, and other non-social groups. Society is still in the stage of inadequate provision for the consequences of existing evils. Larger sums are asked each year for the care of defectives; science is becoming more skillful in picking out and suggesting possible ways of adjusting irresponsibles who are likely to become social charges.[1] Preventive and constructive work must continue to be linked with remedial work.

There is ground for hope that certain of the problems which now loom large will be of less and less importance in the distant future; there is every chance that what

[1] In *Better Times*, October 3, 1927, the statement was made that to keep pace with the increase in the growth of committed insane in the State of New York, a new $12,000,000 hospital must be provided every three years.

has been saved in time and effort in one direction will be diverted into another channel, still with the goal of social welfare in view. It is probable that each succeeding generation will feel responsibility for promoting social change, as the concept of what degree of human happiness can be achieved broadens. Probably the terms "ignorance," "ill-health," "unfortunate incidence of the social system," will still be used, but will in time be descriptive of quite a different state from that to which now applied. The varied meaning which these words have today in different parts of the world indicates that point of view is a variable in determining what social problems are.

Accepting the idea that no society will ever exist which does not acknowledge the presence of problems and does not see the need of a program of social betterment, what is the particular meaning of the term "evils" in twentieth century America? How prevalent are these evils? How persistent are the conditions from which they arise? That definite thing known as "public opinion" determines what are commonly recognized as social problems. No public policy for the treatment of social ills can be developed much in advance of the acceptance of its underlying principles by the popular mind. What then do ignorance, ill-health, economic insecurity mean today?

America reflects a low standard of education in its definition of ignorance; for the term ignorance often means actual illiteracy. Due to our immigration policy of the past fifty years, to our failure to provide an adequate program of adult education, to our reliance upon state and county provision in default of a national education program, to our indifference to educational opportunities for other races than the white, the United States has still a large problem of illiteracy.[2]

Ignorance may mean other things than illiteracy. The foreigner is regarded as ignorant because he is unaware of prevailing customs and ideas; so also is the country man held ignorant when he comes to the city. Ignorance may be said to exist in proportion to the number of persons unaware of and unadapted to the practices of the world in which they live. The adequacy of channels of communication open to all the people largely determines whether or not they are ignorant in this social sense. Ignorance may further mean lack of the particular kind of knowledge needed by the individual facing a certain situation. A young mother is ignorant if she does not know how to care for her child; a structural iron worker is ignorant if he does not know how to handle himself on a steel beam two hundred feet above the ground.

Ignorance is a term which, in common parlance, has both depth and breadth. There are few who are in possession of the facts required to meet crucial individual situations and who are thoroughly equipped with the knowledge of society needed to fit them into their general environment. Illiteracy will certainly be blotted

[2] In the 1920 Census the following figures were given:

Illiterates 21 years or over

		White			Negro
	All Classes	Native Parentage	Foreign or Mixed	Foreign Born	
Number	4,333,111	938,311	102,358	1,707,145	1,512,987
Per Cent	7.1	3.0	0.9	13.7	27.4

The U. S. Census counts those illiterate who cannot write their names.

out as far as the normally intelligent are concerned; methods of communication will continue to improve and to draw all countries and all classes of the population closer together, making it simpler for the individual to know more of the world in which he lives, but also imposing the responsibility of acquiring an ever-widening fund of general information. The work of supplying each individual with the particular facts which he needs has scarcely begun. The success of such an aim is bound up with scientific progress; more exact and more definite methods of distinguishing individual needs and of differentiating the educational process must be provided before the problems of individual life can be successfully met.

Unless an educational technique of a flexibility and efficacy exceeding any present knowledge is developed, it seems probable that ignorance in the social and individual sense will persist. A changing society must of necessity produce those incapable of keeping up with the vanguard. Methods of meeting situations often develop after experience with the situation, not simultaneously. The concept of a society which will have a solution at hand for every contingency that arises seems remote from reality.

Mental and physical ill health are probably given as much attention in the United States as elsewhere in the world; also, a great amount of preventive work is being done. Yet, there is no other country with so high an accident rate,[3] and none where the tension of modern

[3] "The latest available figures for the United States which can be compared with those of other countries are for 1924. In that year in the United States Registration States there occurred 76.2 fatal accidents per 100,000

life is said to produce greater nervous disorganization. Some question whether the health of the population has been materially improved during the past fifty years; they assert that advances in medical knowledge and treatment merely balance the increase in factors of disintegration. Positive evidence of increased longevity cannot be supplied from mortality tables. They are frequently interpreted to prove that adult man's expectancy of life is greater than formerly, but they show much more clearly that infant and child mortality has been so cut that average life expectancy has been increased. The middle-aged man seems no surer of living to ripe old age than he formerly did.[4]

Though there were definite proof of increased longevity, little assurance would be given of greater health during life. The attainment of old age may mean merely advance in methods of deferring death—that is, ill health rendered less fatal—and does not of itself suggest that humanity is benefited.

The amount of time lost from work on account of sickness each year by the average citizen,[5] the number of permanent patients in hospitals for the insane, feeble-minded, and defective, the ever-increasing amounts expended upon health education indicate that mental and physical ill health are social problems of magnitude.

population. In England and Wales during the same year, the death rate for all accidents was only 34.1 per 100,000 of population." *Report of the Committee on Public Accident Statistics, 1926*, p. 3 (National Safety Council, Chicago, 1926).

[4] Dublin, "The Economics of World Health," *Harper's Magazine*, November, 1926.

[5] Estimates vary on this from an approximate annual loss of 13 days, computed by Fisher of Yale in 1909, to the more recent figures of 7 to 9 days per year, computed by Dublin and Frankel of the Metropolitan Life Insurance Company.

As to the persistence of the causes of ill health, little is known as to man's ability to perfect his physical make-up under ideal conditions. In fact, few would venture to describe conditions which could be guaranteed as ideal. At present, there is no end in sight of the need of efforts to improve individual health.

In discussing ignorance and ill health in present-day life, there has been some suggestion of the part played by economic and social organization in creating these evils. The third evil, "the unfortunate incidence of the present social system," is inclusive, at least partially, of the two first-named evils. Our immigration policy was late in developing clear principles and has been responsive to demands based on the economic advantage of American manufacturers, as well as to the need of a new country for settlers and the need of many Europeans for a freer political life and more physical space than were offered at home. Our failure to meet the social situation caused by the introduction of large numbers of foreigners into American communities has often been due to our absorption in individual profit-making and short-sightedness in matters of public welfare. Lack of national educational standards has resulted in inequality of opportunity for the population in general, where race prejudice, local poverty, or indifference exist. Failure to develop a nation-wide educational program may be ascribed to the absence of a national philosophy, to the prevalence of an individualistic economy which emphasizes respect for private property, and to a federal system of government which leaves to the individual states most of the responsibility for handling local problems. Low wages, long hours, unemployment, bad housing, and unwholesome conditions of work for a long time seemed to be the lot of the ignorant and of the unassimilated foreigner. Mental and physical ill health were natural corollaries of poor living and working conditions.

When profit-making is the accepted objective of economic organization the test of efficiency is not usually stated in terms of social welfare. Only where public opinion or state policy is based on an explicit idea of social values to be protected is there thought to be reason for placing checks upon privately controlled activities. Legislation as to conditions of employment, physical surroundings, safety devices, compensation for injuries, working hours, minimum wages, holidays, etc., has been framed and enforced by the state. Such legislation must win support by gradually disarming prejudices due to the individualism of the population, and must, as a rule, reflect conditions which are already in effect to a considerable extent.

More immediately effective than legislation is the awakening of individual managers to the advantages resulting from improved economic conditions for their workers. Strong evidence has accumulated that a leaven is at work which necessitates less pressure from without to enforce recognition of social problems. Either because there is a conviction that a prosperous, well-educated society is good for business, or because there is belief that new principles for directing economic progress are in order, an impetus towards improvement of working and general living conditions is coming from business men themselves. Personnel and efficiency engineering, the influence of collegiate schools of business are bearing fruits. The business man frequently wishes to bring about changes in his own way; individualism is evident in his unwillingness to allow the state or organized labor to direct his good impulses, though he sponsors the idea that the state should enact legislation to protect his economic interests—viz., a protective tariff, protection of foreign investments, blue-sky laws. But extension of legislation, or of union dictation, to such problems as irregular employment, old age and health insurance, compensation for industrial disease, meet with opposition from the enlightened employer who takes good care of his workmen, as well as from those who wish to sidestep their responsibilities.

The uncontrolled momentum of industrial progress is as important as the profit incentive in producing dislocation of social interests. The automobile has been of incalculable benefit and pleasure to the modern world, but who foresaw and made provision for the congestion in traffic, the increase in accidents, the changes in home life which have resulted from it? Our industrial program has taken little account of social consequences as conquest over material objects has been achieved. Industry has shaped the world and has put terrific pressure upon certain parts of the social structure. Adjustment is called for, but adjustment of such fundamental nature as to involve dislocation.

It seems inevitable that progress shall bring difficult social situations in its train. Men will be thrown out of work when there is no demand for the products of a certain factory. Time will be necessary to fit them into new positions, and society alone is responsible for making the transition as painless as possible. The strike in the woolen and worsted mills of Passaic, New Jersey, during 1926-27, illustrates how futile it is to expect individuals to adjust their differences when immediate personal interests run counter to social situations. Back of the mill-owners' refusal to maintain the old wage scale was the fact that they faced a diminishing market for their goods, due to public preference for silk rather than woolen products and to changed habits as to amount of clothing worn. Back of the workers' refusal to accept a wage cut was realization that life is not worth much when standards of decency cannot be maintained. There seemed no satisfactory solution in the hands of the individuals involved. In the name of common humanity, food and clothing were supplied the strikers, but society offered no help with the fundamental problem.

In Great Britain the coal strike of 1926 furnished a vivid instance of the lack of social control in the face of an acute industrial crisis. Many of the essential facts seem to have been admitted by both sides; the issue of opposing interests was squarely faced, but there seemed no power in society to decide which side should yield. In fact, society is frequently uncertain as to how the general welfare can best be served. No program of social control with government authority and backed by the will of the people is in existence. Even the principles upon which such a program could be based are lacking. Social scientists have not gone far enough in study of practical situations to have established themselves as advisers; few of them are equipped to counsel upon the varied problems involved in an industrial situation. They are frequently specialists upon one aspect of social life and have not the knowledge or perspective to cope with a given social situation in its entirety.

Ignorance, ill health, and the unfortunate incidence of social progress seem serious and persisting elements in modern society. Granting this, what part does social work play in meeting the situation? Those who promote and those who engage in social service appear to recognize two objectives:

1. The adjustment of individuals and groups to their environment.
2. The improvement of conditions which make adjustment difficult for many persons.

The accomplishment of either objective is dependent upon the accomplishment of the other. On the face of the matter, it is evident that at times the individual must be fitted to the situation and at other times the situation must be changed to fit the individual. Common sense indicates that any practical plan for improving social welfare must balance these two methods of bringing about adjustment.

The social worker undoubtedly strives to strike such a balance when handling any particular case—the environment is made as favorable as possible for the changing of personality, health, and behavior of the client in the direction desired. Frequently the social worker finds himself up against an almost insoluble problem in trying to modify environment to any appreciable degree—if a certain client is to regain his self-respect and the leadership of his household, he must have a job which will yield a decent livelihood. The social worker cannot insure this in a town where unemployment exists in the trade in which the client is skilled. Or perhaps the social worker has to solve a housing problem for a family in a city where there is no provision of the facilities needed at the price which can be paid. When specific medical or educational services which the community cannot supply are required, the social worker is helpless. In such cases much time and effort are expended in making the best of a poor situation.

The second objective of social work cannot conceivably be attained through individual case work. While study of individuals and attack upon the immediate causes of their maladjustment are necessary and valuable in learning general causes of disruption, there must be a direct approach to these general causes. In so far as the individual suffers from the disrupting influences of social and economic life, a satisfactory adjustment cannot be made until there is improvement in the general situation. His problem becomes important because it has an element which is common to the problems of many individuals. Progress in handling the situation will come when the problem of a particular individual is recognized as important because it is representative of the problems of many, and when the sources of the difficulty are sought in the social organization.

Social workers realize, therefore, that the second objective—improvement of conditions causing maladjustment—states the central purpose of the social welfare program. At the same time, under pressure, they would admit that a greater outlay of effort and money is made in helping individuals to get along under present conditions than in seeking to change those conditions. why is this the case?

First, the term "social welfare program" in common parlance does not cover programs in education, health, and recreation which are primarily concerned with the constructive work of improving individual and social environment. The social welfare program is intended to provide for the helpless, the defective, the diseased, and other non-social groups. The opportunities for working with normal people, under normal conditions, are preempted by other programs bearing other names. Yet, as pathology in medicine has yielded valuable data upon health, so the handling of non-social groups is expected to throw light upon society in general. The conditions which cause maladjustment among individuals not well equipped socially may also be responsible for slowing down the rate of general social progress. When the remedy is found for treating the disease, the same remedy may be used as a general tonic for those who have no specific disease. The need of analyzing the pathological condition in relation to the whole organism—society—and of considering the effect of treatment upon the organism is essential. The social welfare program fails to live up to its name if it fails to take account of this responsibility.

Second, the most obvious and immediate way of helping those in distress is to seek to solve individual problems. This usually means that attention is concentrated on doing the best one can in a given situation.

The demands upon social workers are apt to be importunate, the needs to be met are acute. It is more than natural that energy and money should be absorbed by emergent individual problems, as long as energy and money are limited in amount.

Third, little opportunity is given social workers to do more than meet acute individual situations, because the public has a limited concept of the goal to be set for a social welfare program. There is indefiniteness in the minds of the public as to what tasks and obligations should be allocated to social workers. It is patent that statesmen, educators, health workers, industrial leaders, and others also play a part in shaping and improving social life. On which group does the responsibility rest for seeking out the causes of disruption and dealing with these causes? Or which group is best situated strategically for striking at the roots of existing ills? These questions have not been satisfactorily answered, and, consequently, social workers are neither expected nor desired to study fundamental reasons for distress and to evolve a program for reconstruction. There would be little public sympathy for the assumption of such a task, and financial support would certainly not precede sympathetic understanding.

Fourth, the reluctance of the public to assign responsibility for changing social conditions may not be due so much to lack of confidence in the ability of these various groups to bring about changes, as to uncertainty of the advisability of attempting to change existing conditions. Difference of opinion as to what is the cause of social ills, and even as to the definition of ills, makes a general welfare program a highly controversial subject. While the majority would hold that ignorance of health rules, of a trade, of social living was an evil, there would be little agreement upon the way of combatting such ignorance. The difficulty which is encountered in enforcing compulsory school attendance for children, and the arguments which have defeated a national amendment prohibiting child labor, attest to the divergence of opinion upon the value of education in preventing ignorance.

In the same way good health for every one is an accepted ambition, but whether the means of achievement is to be through eugenics, birth control, compulsory health examinations and treatment is not yet determined. Nor is there any very definite standard set up which makes explicit the term "good health."

When an attempt is made to define what the minimum economic standards of life should be, even more difficulties are encountered. The U. S. Bureau of Labor Statistics has set up standards of living for families residing in certain cities. Employers and others question the validity of the standards and challenge the soundness of the basis used—amounts actually expended by families whose schedules were kept. Recognizing that the average family has had little experience in budgeting and has less knowledge of food values, of housing facilities, of the place of recreation, of saving and of other items in an ideal budget, the weakness of the standards set by the Bureau of Labor Statistics is incontestable. Any plan for fixing wages in accordance with such standards meets with considerable opposition.

Unemployment and irregular employment, shut-downs due to industrial strife, occupational diseases, industrial accidents, are all complex disorders of the economic world. Any attempt to meet these ills in the name of social welfare is fraught with danger, since the vested interests of employers and of organized labor must be considered. Intervention even by the state is a delicate matter. Since the world of industry is operated on a profit basis, the stimulus to produce must not be destroyed through the unwise restrictions of government bodies. And yet the labor force of the country must not be exploited to the loss of both individuals and state. How is the right balance to be struck?

Those who support social welfare work are not as a rule sympathetic with attempts to make fundamental changes in the existing economic and social system. Action through the machinery of government or through organizations of labor makes more direct appeal than does social welfare work to those interested in changing social conditions. Social welfare is usually supported by persons who believe that existing conditions are subject to improvement without any radical departure from present institutions and customs. They feel that the existing economic system brings problems in its train, but so would any other system. Their argument is as follows: Such inequalities and sufferings as can be ironed out should be taken care of, but the presence of such evils is no argument for shifting to a new economic basis—such as Socialism or Communism proposes—which would probably be accompanied by even more difficult problems. Social welfare should provide a corrective for the present somewhat faulty system of distribution of the national income, and should take care of those who are unable to be self-supporting under a capitalist—and probably under any other—economic system. As time passes, the need for such assistance should be lessened, as industry becomes more scientifically organized and imbued with a social purpose.[6]

This optimistic belief that evolution will bring forth a satisfactory society without renunciation of the capitalist order and through a gradual modification of existing conditions is supported by many of the economists. Thomas N. Carver in *The Present Economic Revolution in the United States*[7] interprets the present trend towards higher real wages, towards growth of financial power and stock ownership among labor groups, towards coöperation with, instead of war against, capital by organized workers as indicative of the progress of an economic revolution, which will eventuate in a "balanced economic system" with virtual equality of prosperity among occupations. The willingness of labor to share the responsibilities of management and to adapt their union tactics to the promotion of recognized mutual advantages is interpreted by Mr. Carver to mean that the day of warfare between capital and labor is passing.

Social workers appear to adopt a rôle of compromise with the present system. They are criticized for this apparent acceptance of the underlying conditions of social distress and are censured by those who believe

[6] See Siegfried, *America Comes of Age*, chap. III.
[7] See chaps. VII, VIII, IX.

that amelioration simply prolongs the existence of an impossible economic system. Yet it is difficult to see how they could take a different position. Those who feel that the individual can be materially helped only when the entire background of life is changed tend to leave social work and to try some other occupation which sets itself a more concrete task. Those who remain and are successful in social work have an infinite interest in human beings as such, and get their satisfaction out of helping the unfortunate to a larger life. Their interest focuses on individuals, and they can measure the results of their work to some degree. Social work, as at present financed and controlled, seems of necessity to give consideration of the problems of individuals first place. The usefulness of having one group which subordinates every other interest to that of the welfare of the individual would be unquestioned, if other groups were at work upon related problems.

The social worker meets with censure because he applies himself to meeting one aspect—the immediate ills of individuals—of a general social situation, while the other aspects are neglected. Whether such criticism is just must be decided in view of the fact that the social worker is hardly in a position to assume wider responsibilities than he now has. Funds are provided by the public for doing certain jobs and he must respect this confidence. The social worker recognizes a responsibility which extends beyond this concern with the individual. This is stated clearly in the second objective of social work. The question is one of means. If the social worker has neither opportunity nor public acquiescence in changing conditions out of which social ills grow, what part is he to play? His responsibility seems to lie in making known his observations upon general causes of maladjustment and in arousing public interest to the need of measures for dealing with these causes. It may be inadvisable to suggest what should be done about unemployment, for example, but data upon the numbers unemployed, the conditions which appear to grow out of their unemployment, should be forcibly presented. Social workers must collect and analyze their data in form which is usable by other groups.

If statesmen, social scientists, and the public had a social philosophy and an interest in social welfare well developed, the task of the social worker would be direct aid of distressed individuals and presentation of generalized data to the public. But there is the additional function to be discharged of arousing other groups to the need of attack upon social ills. The social scientist and the statesman are seldom prepared to play their parts of studying the causes of maladjustment and of putting into effect plans of prevention and reconstruction. So, the social worker feels called upon to harangue, to expound, to educate the lethargic groups which must be counted upon for coöperation in a welfare program.

The social workers are, therefore, the group which seems cast for the position of leadership in arousing the public to the need of changing certain social conditions. Since they cannot accomplish their task of adjusting individuals unless environment is reasonably favorable, they must do what they can to further an improvement of environment. They must submit to appraisal of their activities towards this end, as well as to appraisal of their other activities. How does social welfare work stand up under this double appraisal?

In regard to the handling of immediate and practical problems of relief, social work has made great progress during the last quarter-century in the United States. Within this period, centralized organization and administration of charities within the state, the county, the municipality have eliminated much of the overlapping, waste, and ineffectiveness which characterized earlier welfare work. The confidential exchange, the community chest, the welfare federation, the council of social agencies, the central information service have each contributed to the unification and adequacy of the welfare program. There is assurance of continuous public support for certain services, such as custodial care of the feeble-minded, the insane, the physically defective and injured. There is general recognition of the claim of the dependent child, the aged, the ill, the ignorant, for assistance from the social group. These battles have been won; hence changes in political parties and personnel no longer determine whether or not welfare programs will be maintained. There are, of course, periods of rapid progress and periods of regression, but the main body of the program is carried on.

Towards the accomplishment of their second objective, social workers have given consistent backing and impetus to social and industrial legislation. Restriction of immigration, factory inspection, housing legislation and inspection, compensation for industrial accidents and diseases, formulation and enforcement of legislation for the protection of women and children, provision of educational opportunities and vocational training at public expense have been initiated and realized to considerable extent through the efforts of social workers.

Though social workers, as an organized group, seldom adopt a formal program of political action and have no specific philosophy as to a desirable social and economic system, they have backed certain measures of social reform with great vigor. They cannot perhaps be counted upon to initiate measures necessary to insure better social conditions, but when such measures are proposed by other groups, social workers will give sympathetic support. If criticism of social work is based upon the unwillingness of social workers to outline a public policy of social welfare, ground for such criticism is admitted. Social workers may counter with the statement that the determination of public policy is the business of statesmen who should use the data offered by scientists, social workers, physicians, educators, industrial engineers and others who are gathering facts about social and industrial life.

In conclusion, it may be said that social workers appear to see their primary function as the application of practical techniques to existing situations. They meet practical situations and confine their efforts to attack upon well-defined evils of present society. They give what time and ingenuity they can afford to dealing with these evils at their source. They expect help and guidance from the statesman and from the social scientist in pointing out the objectives to which a future society may aspire and the means by which these objectives can be realized. Their present program appears to be built along realistic lines and with appreciation of the advantage realized through taking one step at a time along territory known to be stable. Social workers do not live in the belief that they could solve the problems of society if given broader powers and greater financial resources. They admit the need of direction from philosophy and science and perhaps feel that their own contributions are limited by lack of enlightenment and sufficient help from these sources.

It is evident that there is no clear-cut program for a future society, differing from the present, which social work is promoting. At the same time, those who believe that fundamental changes come about through evolutionary processes will see in the constructive methods of social work a sure road to a better social order. In making present society bearable, there must be an attack upon those basic principles from which problems arise. In time, under continued pressure, the old evils may go down, giving place to new social conditions. Some advances can be pointed to which show that the adequate handling of immediate problems may bring about the elimination of the conditions from which they arise. With immigration restricted as at present there will be a permanent diminution in maladjustments due to racial differences and to the overthrow of old standards when Europeans arrive in America.[8]

[8] An exceedingly optimistic view was recently expressed as follows: "If the present immigration policy is maintained . . . we shall have to revise our entire conception of our needs. I predict that within the next ten or twenty years we will see no need for relief for destitution, with industrial conditions as they are at present, and with every able bodied person able to earn a living at good wages." L. K. Frankel, in *New York Times*, Sept. 16, 1926.

Public health work has definitely raised standards of health throughout the country. Compulsory education laws insure school attendance and general literacy. Enlightened business seeks to prevent irregular employment, hazards of work, unwholesome living conditions, insufficient wages.[9]

The rate of progress in achievement of a remedial program and in development of preventive and constructive measures is very uneven in different parts of the United States and even within the states. A city such as Philadelphia may have a sufficient quota of social organizations looking to a well-rounded program, while the surrounding country may be suffering from an almost complete dearth of relief, community, or recreation activities. In the larger towns of the South, one may find Eastern city standards reflected, while in the rural sections there are barbaric conditions—not only social workers unknown, but no physician or registered nurse within a county. The division of responsibility for the care of defectives and delinquents between state and county often results in a fairly adequate provision for a portion of the population and nothing at all for certain other sections.

No judgment may be given upon the effectiveness of present-day social work, except in terms of certain areas. Taking the United States as a whole, one must conclude that the effort to meet existing social evils is ineffective. Within certain cities, as much may be done as anywhere in the world in an attempt to meet the

[9] Irving Fisher in a speech quoted by the *New York Times*, Dec. 12, 1927, prophesied that abject poverty would be eliminated in the United States by 1932, so rapidly are real wages increasing.

social problems arising among an urban population, and yet the situation is not adequately met. In some rural regions slight effort is being made to meet any social problems.[10] The necessity for continuance of the work of mitigating present evils is therefore unquestioned. Even more important is it to discover and deal with the causes of these evils. Social work has recognized both objectives as necessary for social welfare, but addresses itself mainly to remedial work, realizing that assistance from various groups—notably the statesman, the philosopher, and the scientist—must be enlisted, before a thoroughgoing welfare program, which will uproot present evils and will provide for a more satisfactory future society, can be achieved.

---

[10] "The average number of social workers in rural districts throughout the entire country is one to a county." Hurlin, in address before National Conference of Social Work, Cleveland, 1926.

V

CHARACTERISTIC ACTIVITIES
OF SOCIAL WORK

SOCIAL work addresses itself to the persisting social problems mentioned in preceding chapters. These same problems are subject to attack from several angles and the responsibility of directing social change is shared with a number of vocations. Social workers recognize clearly the necessity of coöperating with other groups to secure unity and a well-rounded program, and a unique part is said to be played by social work in coördinating the various programs which seek to promote social welfare. Such coördination implies not only a definite goal in view but some knowledge as to how society may be moulded. How does social work set about this task?

Social workers are fulfilling their natural function when all in the community who are interested in social welfare look to them for assistance. The judge of the juvenile court often has a social worker to collect pertinent data upon each case and to advise as to treatment. A psychiatric social worker becomes an essential member of the staff of the court which commits defectives, dependents, and delinquents to institutional care. Social workers advise the Legislature as to necessary grants for institutions, the prevention of delinquency, crime, and destitution, and the promotion of public welfare. Social legislation is drawn up with their counsel. It is to social workers that the state looks for administration of its public institutions and organizations.

In the field of health the social worker must be at hand for consultation with the doctor and the nurse. Social data are essential for the successful handling of health problems in the clinic, the hospital, the school, the home, or the community. In public health work, combined medical and social knowledge is indispensable. In so far as the social worker has a special skill in collecting social data, he may supplement specialists in physical analysis. The medical profession relies increasingly upon an intimate personal and social history to determine individual treatment of patients.[1]

The social worker is also valued as a specialist in the school. Problems of the classroom can often be solved when information concerning social background is supplied. The new position of "visiting teacher" is coming to be recognized as essential in up-to-date schools. The visiting teacher is primarily a social case worker.

Those who are misfits in industry may become adjusted when the social worker links up knowledge of home conditions with the work situation. Personnel departments are finding that visits to the home must supplement interviews on the job.

In the church there is a double reason for relying upon the social worker, since there is not only the usual

[1] Recently the physician in charge of a thoroughly modern university hospital and medical school ready to open announced he was unwilling to receive patients until he was assured of an adequate department of social service in the hospital.

desire to serve, but also desire to give spiritual guidance. Neither purpose can be achieved without a thorough understanding of individual social problems. The church is requiring more and more straight social work training for those leading its activities.

In the instances enumerated, the social worker is definitely associated with those in other fields of work and the chief idea is to supplement and render effective their activities. Many other illustrations could be given. Often the social worker is used to aid the community with a recreation program, to make suggestions as to housing regulations, to give pointers to the architect upon tenement planning or to the landowner upon a possible level of rentals, to explain racial food habits and prejudices to the home economist, and so on. There seems no field which the social worker may not touch more or less directly.

There is a large area of activity where an individual worker is not supplementing the program of others, but where he is carrying out his own program. What do these characteristic activities comprise? The largest and best-defined province of social work is *case work*. Most of those social workers mentioned above as supplementing work in other fields are applying a case work technique, which has been acquired in the field of social work proper. There are case-working organizations, commonly known as family welfare, or child welfare societies, maintained on private funds in practically every city of the United States. Child welfare agencies are engaged in the care of dependent, delinquent, defective, and abnormal children in their homes, in school, in court, and in institutions. Family

welfare agencies center their attention upon the family
as a unit, seeking to rehabilitate or improve families
not adjusted to their social environment, on account
of physical, racial, or economic difficulties. In addition,
there are frequently departments of the city and
county government, supported by taxation, which
engage in case work.

A second group, closely allied with case workers, includes those in *charge of institutions*, public and private,
for the care of the indigent, the dependent, the insane,
the feeble-minded, the criminal, the delinquent, the af-
flicted. Successful handling requires individual case
studies and records not unlike those of the social case
agencies. The institution worker has fewer resources
to draw upon in bringing about an adjustment, but,
at the same time, he has such resources as are available
under more complete control. Unfortunately, many
institution workers are so engrossed with administrative
responsibilities and the practical business of feeding and
clothing their charges that they do not get far with their
case studies.

A third characteristic field of social work is *community organization*, which includes a variety of health,
educational, recreational, civic activities designed to
prevent maladjustment and to build up social unity.
In this category fall the settlement houses (now usually
called neighborhood or community houses), the Y. M.
C. A., the Y. W. C. A., the Boy Scouts, the various
clubs, camps and other recreational activities which
are organized along non-commercial lines. The work
of public health officers, the county agent, the home
demonstrator, the public health nurse, the Red Cross

social worker, the public welfare county superintendent may all be primarily concerned with creating and directing community programs.

A fourth field of social work is that of *coördination and planning* of welfare programs. Community chests, federations of agencies, confidential exchanges, city, county, and state councils of social agencies, and other organizations which draw together the various social agencies, interpret their programs to the public, and obtain financial support, constitute a distinct field of activity.

A fifth division is *social legislation and research,* which embraces to some extent those engaged in the collection of data and the promotion of programs striking at recognized evils in the present social organization. The Children's Bureau, the Women's Bureau, national and state bureaus of labor statistics, organizations to promote social legislation, research departments within social agencies and institutions make up this group.

A sixth division of the field is *public welfare administration.* Superintendents of state, county, and city welfare departments have functions and responsibilities somewhat different from those of the other groups. They are case workers, as they often receive wards of the court, place dependent children, act as probation and parole officers, etc. They are institutional workers, must understand problems of finance and management, and must supervise and inspect all public institutions. They are community organizers and have as a primary responsibility the development and coördination of a public welfare program. They also promote and enforce legislation, collect and present data to the public and to governmental bodies for their guidance and general enlightenment. Besides these various duties the public welfare administrator is expected to lead the community to a broader concept of the rôle the state may play in creating a happier society.

Social agencies of the types mentioned are constantly seeking the aid of such other specialists as the physician, the educator, the legislator, the architect, the home economist, the public health nurse, just as these latter use the social worker to supplement their programs. There is a real interest in determining whether there is a legitimate and continuing reason for regarding social work as a vocation with exclusive problems and with a technique for which special educational provision must be made, or whether the problems are common to many groups, which may solve them independently and individually. How is one to determine when social work is being carried on, or when some other activity has a social work approach or aspect?

In an address before the National Conference of Social Work in 1915, Mr. Abraham Flexner discussed the question of social work's claim to being a profession and came to a decisive negative conclusion. He found it impossible to draw a clear line of demarcation about the field of social work as can be done for medicine, law, architecture, engineering. It was suggested that social work was "not so much a definite field, as an aspect of work in many fields,"[2] and that social work has grown up to supply the shortcomings of the pro-

---

[9] "Is Social Work a Profession?" *Studies in Social Work*, No. 4, (The New York School of Philanthropy), p. 17.

fessions, whose development may not yet be completed. Not only does Mr. Flexner find lack of specific aim and responsibility in social work, but he discovers another discrepancy in necessary standards for a profession: the possession of "a technique capable of communication through an orderly and highly specialized educational discipline"[3] is naturally lacking, since social work has been unable to define its aims clearly.

Many social workers disagreed with Mr. Flexner's conclusion that social work had no definite field apart from the professions and with his belief that it was unlikely to develop into a full profession. Perhaps as many agreed that social work was not yet a profession but believed that it would become one; a few thought that it was not a profession and not likely to become one but felt that the question was relatively unimportant. Certainly, the majority of social workers regarded Mr. Flexner's statement as a challenge and have directed their energies during the past ten years toward the achievement of professional status.

At the National Conference of Social Work in 1925, the President of the American Association of Social Workers re-examined Mr. Flexner's appraisal of social work in terms of certain stated tests of a profession. Representing an organization which owes its existence to a belief that social work is a profession, Mr. Hodson claimed that social work had definite aims and in case work had developed a technique capable of transmission through a specialized educational discipline.[4]

[3] *Ibid*, p. 7.
[4] "Is Social Work Professional?" *Proceedings of the National Conference of Social Work*, 1925. pp. 629-36.

It was further claimed that in community and group work the social worker is doing a highly specialized job capable of definition and description. He concluded, however, that public opinion offers the final test of professional status and that social work has probably not yet attained such standing in the popular mind.

There are a number of reasons why it is important to determine the status of social work. While it may be argued that it is unimportant whether or not social work is termed a profession, providing that its activities are carried on efficiently and in the genuine professional spirit, conditions which must be met to establish social work as a profession may also be indispensable for insuring that its activities are efficiently pursued. Mr. Flexner pointed out that social work is of intellectual character and of complex pattern, due to its task of supplementing other vocations wherever necessary. Unless there is a certain province recognized as proper to social work, and unless its activities can be described and defined, how is it possible for social work to supplement work in other fields without either overlapping or confusing? If it is true that the professions—law, medicine, education, government—are developing and changing, how can social work accept so vague a task as supplementing them in whatever way is necessary? Preparation for so large and undefined a range of activities seems incredibly difficult; yet, as was indicated above, only careful preparation could enable a social worker to be useful and not a nuisance. The fundamental basis for a specialized educational discipline seems lacking, if objectives can be stated only in general terms, and if there is need of training in widely diverse methods for attack upon an indefinite number of problems.

Is the above description of social work as lacking definite objectives and a definite field of its own, fair? Certainly social workers themselves feel that social work plays a rôle quite distinct from its function of supplementing the work of other vocations. And this point of view is understandable when attention is focused upon the individual who invokes the aid of the social worker, rather than upon the relationship of social work to any one of the professions. As was suggested in the first chapter, social work views the individual as an entity and seeks to bring all the resources of the community to bear upon his problems. The most important function of the social worker, and certainly the function which seems most exclusively his, is to see that his client gets the benefit of everything offered by the community. To know what remedies should be applied to a case, and to know how and where these remedies are obtainable, seems a task of no small responsibility, calling for thorough knowledge of both the client and the community, combined with skill in adaptation. The social worker may be likened to the general practitioner of medicine who has a definite pharmacopoeia upon which he draws for the treatment of his patient. Perhaps more rests in the hands of the physician, since he may with greater ease vary the drugs administered and may experiment with combinations; the social worker summons aid from another person and immediately shares a certain part of the responsibility for the case. The analogy holds, though, when the physician calls upon the oculist, the surgeon, and other specialists to provide for adequate treatment of his patient.

The social worker is the person to whom the client looks for advice upon all possible sources of relief—medical, physical, legal, educational, recreational, economic—which the community affords. It is certainly no one else's function to supply such advice, and the reasons are obvious why, in a complex society, there is great advantage in having such advice centralized. A strong case could be made for the support of social work if it could be shown that a complete and discriminating appraisal of community resources was being made available to all who were in need of it. The public has not yet recognized that the supplying of accurate information regarding the community is a necessary and distinct kind of service. Social workers have not assumed, to any important degree, the rôle of counselor as divorced from the giving of a certain kind of relief. Usually the social worker comes as the representative of an organization which is one of the sources of material aid within the community upon which the client may draw. Sometimes the organization is prepared to give concrete commodities; sometimes there is budget-planning for the household, or provision for recreational or educational facilities, or service in the form of companionship and personal direction.

As long as there is little understanding of the value of supplying accurate information concerning social resources and of a program based upon such knowledge, there is little likelihood that special financial provision

will be made for such service. The social worker will, of
necessity, combine the function of social information
expert with some other function. The client will apply
for help to a social organization known to offer services
of a definite character; the contributor will subscribe
to organizations which promise to show results of a
tangible kind with a minimum of the funds going to
overhead expenses. Unless the social worker proclaims
his service as a specialist in knowledge of the community and defends it as a primary, and not a second-
ary, function, the process of coördinating all social
resources for the benefit of individual citizens will be
long deferred.

Before the social worker can convince others of the
importance of his counseling function, he must have a
clear case to present. This means that he must show the
urgency of the need for sound counsel and his own
peculiar fitness to supply this need. To the present
time, it must be admitted that he has given more time
to explaining and defending his active function as a
dispenser of certain services than to emphasizing the
activities of counselor. A strong argument could undoubtedly be made for creating a group which will act
as a coördinating agency, bringing into line the various
factors bearing upon social welfare. It is obvious that
there would be an attempt to fill in gaps exposed, and
eventually the formulation of an integrated social
program would follow the analysis of existing social
services. Already social workers have taken steps in
setting their own house in order—i.e., they have created
welfare federations, councils of social agencies, confidential exchanges, which have made unified pro-

grams for the relief, recreational, health, and educational work carried on by social organizations proper. At the same time, there has been advance in organization of health councils and of educational councils providing for unity of program in groups closely related to the social work agencies.

A good background has been provided for those who are interested in drawing various welfare programs together in order to fashion a general plan for social welfare. Society is often described as a complex mechanism. It is unlike most modern machinery in that no work-model of it is at hand; no person accepts the responsibility of understanding all its parts. If attention is focused on a particular section, the verdict may be: "What a splendid piece of construction!" A closer inspection may reveal that the products are interference and confusion, since this very part is geared too high for interaction with other parts. Such coördination as has been achieved in social mechanism appears to have come about through wearing down by friction, not by the fitting of one part to another according to a definite pattern. It is as though a fabricated ship were built without a design being drawn—each manufacturer being told to make as good a model as possible of a certain necessary part of a ship. Little of the advantages of specialization can be realized under such conditions.

There is no section of the government which has the authority to unify the programs of the various professions and to supervise privately controlled organizations. It is doubtful if the time will come to delegate to a government body alone the delicate task of making an adequate social program. There must be extensive experiment to determine what are the ingredients in a desirable social program, how they should be combined, and how the results can be successfully tested.

The social worker is now prepared to undertake only a limited rôle in social coördination—to indicate exactly what is being done for social welfare and to point out where noticeable gaps occur. It does not seem premature to mention at this time the suitability of the social worker for the task of supplying information upon community resources to those seeking it. The urgency for meeting such a need is assumed to have been shown in an earlier chapter, which dealt with the persisting social problems necessitating a complex welfare program. At the beginning of this chapter it was shown how the social worker applies himself to supplementing other vocations, and how, from study of the individual, he develops an independent program supplying needs neglected by others. Presumably, it is proper for the social agency to plan for a client only after ascertaining all possible services open to him. The social worker must plan to use these services as effectively as possible, and will never create a new type of service unless existing resources are inadequate. The more ingenuity shown in assembling aid from existing sources, the higher the standard of work done. Granted, then, that the social worker must study all social welfare aspects of other professions, is instrumental in developing such aspects, and is constantly engaged in combining the services offered by all other fields, the fitness of the social worker to advise on community resources seems established. No other professional has gone as far in studying possible interrelationships with other fields. No other group seems so well qualified for extending the present service of individual and community counseling, which is even now of prime importance. Social workers must explain the essential nature of this service to arouse general appreciation of the value of work already being done and interest in its expansion.

VI

SOCIAL WORK INTERPRETED
BY THE SOCIAL WORKER

IF social workers are not emphasizing their value as specialists in advice upon community resources, what is the primary claim which they advance for public support? What do they themselves feel that they are accomplishing? One looks to their literature and official statements for explanation. Members of the faculties of schools of social work, officials of the national associations of social workers, and staff members of social welfare organizations may be regarded as spokesmen for the group; the programs, subsequently published, of the National Conference of Social Work, pronunciamentos of the American Association of Social Workers and of the Association of Schools of Professional Social Work, publications for which social workers are directly responsible, may be expected to reflect group interests and objectives.

A number of attempts have recently been made by the professional group to define social work and to analyze its activities. The American Association of Social Workers is issuing a series of bulletins upon the vocational aspects of several divisions of social work. There have been a few books published dealing specifically with case work or containing first-hand case histories; others have dealt with community organization, the settlement house, immigration, problems of delinquency, publicity methods, etc. Several books have appeared upon the general field of social work, its historical development, the present trends in education and training.[1] In addition, numerous books in the fields of psychology, political science, sociology, and economics discuss problems of social welfare and their treatment. Then, there are periodicals which record current happenings in the fields of social welfare and applied sociology, with articles of more or less technical nature.

It would seem that through these channels the public might receive any enlightenment desired upon the purposes and accomplishments of social work. But very little of this printed matter ever reaches those who support social work. Most of it is intended for the class room—either for students in schools of social work or in university classes in the social sciences. Much else that is published—the monthly publications of the social organizations, for instance—is intended for internal consumption by social workers themselves. The discussions of social work which combine case histories with a good narrative style, important biographical or historical material sometimes reach the public. No field has a richer vein of "human interest" upon which to draw than social work, both because each case has a personal element, and because the universality of the problems presented compels attention.

It is questionable, however, whether selected case studies, chosen to illustrate the existence of certain problems and the use of certain methods, can give the reader an understanding of social work as a whole.

[1] See Bibliography, the *Social Work Series* of the Russell Sage Foundation.

Often the cases are selected because they are interesting and have been well handled, rather than because they are representative of work being generally done. Analysis of a large number of cases and conclusions as to possible standards for the treatment of typical cases have not yet been produced. In fact, writers and speakers emphasize the necessarily individual character of each case and see danger in the adoption of a definite technique. It is stated with decision that there is no common element in the treatment of deserted families, for example, as there may be in treatment of cases of pneumonia or appendicitis. Those who are urging the publication of material suitable for teaching purposes seem to believe that necessary technical standards will be evolved through general acceptance of a definite procedure in record writing, classification of data, and analysis of treatment.

Possibly the chief reason that social work has not been explained to the public is that it is not yet in form to be explained. It was said earlier that the underlying assumptions of the stated social work program are (1) possession of knowledge as to what would be desirable social conditions and (2) knowledge as to how the behavior of human beings can be molded into new form. How clear is the claim of social work to having established these premises?

Utopias have been pictured by reformers, those interested in government or in social welfare, from an early day—as early as our written records of the past. In the majority of these formulas for an ideal society, no transition is provided from the present time, and no consideration given the fact that the same inhabitants of the same world must carry through the plans outlined. Developments within the last century in psychology and in historical interpretation of past events have led to greater conservatism in predicting wholesale social improvement within a short space of time. It does not seem profitable to describe a society cut from new and whole cloth with none of the complexities and characteristics of existing conditions. In the United States less is said than formerly as to the ultimate goal towards which reformers are aiming. The next step is suggested and not much beyond—to cut down the death rate from tuberculosis, from heart disease, from accidents, is the immediate object of public health work; to improve wages, stabilize employment, stimulate production and consumption is the aim of those who wish to improve economic conditions.

In social welfare programs there is the same tendency to suggest concrete next steps rather than to block out a picture of future society. So long as the program calls for decent housing, recreational facilities, adequate food and clothing, universal education, diminution in crime and delinquency, protection of health, there is a specific enough basis for asking support from the public; though the social worker makes no attempt to picture an ideal order of society to which the accomplishment of these minimum social needs may be a stepping stone. Common-sense standards of what are desirable social conditions are accepted.

A more definite statement is made with respect to the social worker's ability to improve conditions through influencing human behavior. This second premise of social work rests upon confidence in the efficacy of social case work. The social worker today seems committed to the belief that individual case work must precede and accompany the solution of social problems. Work for the community is built upon understanding of individual problems. The weight of the social work program lies back of the case work approach to social problems. Attack upon the underlying general conditions of unemployment, protective legislation, pressure of urban life and so forth,[2] seems less the business of the social worker than the adjustment of individuals to these conditions.

Social case work is one instrument by which human behavior is said to be modified. This, the central and most characteristic activity of social work, is defined by one of its leading exponents as consisting of "those processes which develop personality through adjustments, consciously effected, individual by individual, between men and their social environment." The processes which make up treatment are further analyzed under two heads—"insight" and "acts"; "insight into individuality and personal characteristics," and "acts" displayed in "direct action of mind upon mind" and "indirect action through the social environment."[3] This definition is not readily understood by the layman, since familiar terms are used in a rather specific sense. Interpreted broadly, it states that case work accomplishes the adjustment of individuals to their social environment through the knowledge which the social worker possesses both of the individual and of his social situation. Such knowledge is used to influence

[2] See chaps. I and II.
[3] Richmond, *What is Social Case Work?* pp. 98-101.

the individual in a desired direction and to shape the circumstances of his life so that a more favorable environment is provided.

The case worker is here claiming to do much more than assemble community resources and advise the client upon their use. Exhaustive knowledge of human characteristics and of the effects of environment upon individuals, knowledge of how the mind of the specialist may act directly upon the mind of the client, and of how social environment can be used to develop the personality of the client, form the necessary basis for the treatment undertaken. The majority of social workers seem ready to rest their aspirations for professional status upon their claim to having created an important technique of universal significance in dealing with human problems. If they are able to effect personality development in the ways suggested above, they have indeed an instrument of inestimable value to society. The validity of these claims must be examined.

What kind of educational background enables the social worker to bring a penetrating insight to bear upon the social environment and upon individual human characteristics? The answer at once given is that educational preparation affects only indirectly the case worker's skill. Leading social workers state definitely that there are no university subjects which can be designated as indispensable.[4] Some state strong preferences for sociology, economics, political science, psychology, history; others feel that a broad liberal

[4] Bruno, Conference of the Association of Schools of Professional Social Work, New York, December, 1925.

arts course with emphasis upon literature and the languages may be a better foundation.[5] In schools of social work one finds considerable diversity of subject matter in view of the common objective of preparation for a specialized field. When case work is specifically taught, the usual method is to give as much field work as possible, since the accepted belief is that skill is acquired by doing. Much discussion goes on as to how class work may be most effectively combined with field work, so that the group, rather than the individual, may set up standards of evaluation. It is generally conceded that skill in personality adjustment can only be acquired through experience, while capacities of the individual, out of which skill is developed, may be brought forth and increased through class-room work.

In teaching case work, the schools attempt to synthesize and condense what is usually acquired through years of experience on the job. It seems fair to conclude that in essence case work is an art rather than a science. More seems to depend upon the personality and native abilities of the practitioner than upon assimilation of intellectual concepts. Perhaps this will only hold true until the underlying concepts of case work have been made more explicit. Several analyses of case work technique recently made are steps in this direction.[6]

[5] "Training for family social work can be secured in a school of social work or as an apprentice in one of the family societies. There is a marked tendency to limit entrance to either type of training course to college graduates. A well-rounded college curriculum affording a broad cultural education is regarded as the best preparation for training in family case work rather than a course of study too closely related to the social sciences." *Vocational Aspects of Family Social Work.* American Assn. of Social Workers, New York, 1926, p. 22.

[6] See Bibliography.

Lack of uniformity in the educational equipment of case workers who are regarded as successful gives proof that a definite educational preparation does not explain the acquisition of ability to handle personality adjustments. Before 1908 there was little opportunity for training for social work except by apprenticeship; only since 1918 has there been emphasis upon preparation in a school of social work. For several years past, the schools have produced annually about four hundred graduates from one and two year courses of markedly different content. Estimates range from 8,000 to 21,000[7] of those who are incontestably social workers carrying on work above clerical or routine grade: case workers of all kinds—family, child, psychiatric, medical—visiting teachers, probation officers, executives of social organizations, publicity and research workers, staff members of criminal and social welfare institutions, superintendents of public welfare, faculties of schools of social work, community organizers, club and recreation workers. Though there are no dependable figures on general turnover, a conservative estimate of new positions to be filled annually is ten per cent of all positions in the field.[8] Even these approximate figures indicate that only a small proportion of those in the field could have had any specific academic preparation for social work.

[7] See footnote, p. 122.

[8] At the National Conference of Social Work, Cleveland, 1926, Ralph Hurlin summarized recent studies on annual turnover in social work, giving estimates varying from 26% to 34%. A study made of the New York Charity Organization Society staff showed that of those in its employ on a given day, 50% had left after 9 months; after a year 60% had left; after two years only 16% remained.

A study begun in 1922 by the American Association of Social Workers and completed in 1926 by the Russell Sage Foundation offers certain data upon the educational background and professional training of social workers.[9] Questionnaires from 1,258 social workers, representing 677 organizations in 221 cities of the United States, have been tabulated and yield the following facts:

	Men	Women
Per cent with full college education.........	60	40
Per cent with one year or more school of social work education.................	9	15
Per cent with full college and full school of social work education.................	7	7
Per cent with no college and no school of social work education.................	15	20

1,030 schedules were from women, 228 from men; so the figures indicating the educational preparation of women are the more valuable in reflecting the general status of social workers. The proportion of men to women in the field is usually estimated at about one to ten.

Certainly here is proof that the case worker is not usually fitted for his task because of specialized educational preparation. Knowledge of psychology, economics, sociology, social legislation, does not appear to be stressed in the educational preparation of the social worker. Further inquiry must be made as to how the

[9] This study is unpublished and hereafter will be referred to as the Russell Sage Study of 1922, in distinction to the Russell Sage Study of 1925, which is also an unpublished collection of statistics. Parts of the 1922 Study have been incorporated in articles by Ralph Hurlin appearing in *The Survey* in 1926.

social worker comes by his dependable fund of information in regard to the individual and the social environment. What is the unique quality of the social worker's experience from which a definite technique for adjusting personality is developed?

The social worker is in intimate relationship with certain individuals who, ordinarily, apply for assistance when facing an acute personal problem of economic, legal, medical, ethical, or psychological nature. Personal problems present an infinite variety of aspects, and the social worker is called upon to exercise his ingenuity and the full resources of the community in order to achieve adjustments. He must be able to assemble all the facts which are pertinent and must be able to hold the confidence of all with whom he deals through his evident knowledge of facts. In addition, he must inspire confidence by other than rational methods of treatment. The client must develop some emotional responsiveness to the adviser if there is to be any personality growth. The creation of such reactions involves activities of an intellectual and subtle order. Still, it is not apparent how such activities differ from those of others who seek to mold human conduct and to solve personal problems.

The personnel director in an industrial establishment is sometimes regarded as a social worker but more often has the background and the associations of a psychologist, an industrial engineer, or a business man. He is a case worker within a certain sphere as surely as is the social case worker. His progress-card for employees is not unlike the face-card of the social welfare organization; his job analyses, production studies, promotion charts, educational programs, welfare and recreational projects supply him with specialized data upon the individual and his environment. He knows how to develop and control his employees through environment; his tactics in meeting personnel problems within the industry are based upon knowledge of these facts.

In much the same way the dean of a college gathers individual data upon each student and builds up a body of facts which determines policies in general, as well as specific treatment of individuals. Both the dean and the personnel director have as their main activity the study of individuals and their environment with the idea of bringing about the best possible adjustment. Numerous instances could be cited where definite case work is done by those who rely upon it to accomplish a more general aim than individual adjustment—the business executive needs much social knowledge and skill in leading human beings; so does the football coach, the teacher, and the minister.

The social case worker functions swiftly and surely within a certain sphere—a sphere which is chiefly limited to work with those who have a narrow economic margin if any, and who are unable, because of ignorance, to avail themselves of the community's resources for self-adjustment. It seems unlikely that the social worker has acquired a general technique for dealing with social problems which would enable him to function equally well as guide and counselor to students of an undergraduate college, as personnel director in an industry, or as a supervisor of delinquent boys. There appears no basis for the claim to a general technique in personality adjustments, so long as the social worker states that his skill is acquired from "doing," and this "doing" is limited to a certain section of the population whose problems represent only a portion of the problems of society.

Social case work is not conceded, therefore, to have any unique quality. The technique that has been built up is apparently not the product of any educational discipline to which social workers have submitted, but is based upon experience with certain types of social problems. The technique thus evolved is of value in enabling the case worker to carry a large number of cases and to handle skillfully a wide range of problems encountered by that portion of the population which has an economic handicap or is ignorant of community resources. This is a work of great importance and is essential to the social welfare.

It seems relatively unimportant to emphasize the fact that social work cannot establish professional status by offering the technique of case work as proof that it has an exclusive field. What can be accomplished by good case work is of great social value; first, the solution of problems of individuals who may be suffering or who may be causing injury to society; and, second, the development of a scientific attitude towards individual problems, which will ultimately produce a technique capable of being analyzed for the enlightenment of all interested in problems of human behavior. This technique will be created through developing scientific methods of careful observation and of collection of data, through planning based on inductive analysis of pertinent facts, and through systematizing and generalizing procedure. Social workers in the natural course of their jobs have access to material of great potential value to the social sciences; putting this material into form which would meet the needs of the social sciences should be an important function of social work.

Issue has been taken with the attitude of social workers that their greatest contribution to society is the development of the case-work method. Case work is the method by which the social worker may put to practical use his knowledge of community resources. Granted that there is particular skill acquired by the case worker through long experience in developing personality and in bringing about adjustments to social environment, this important type of social service seems no more essential than that of assembling data upon community resources. This latter function, which the social worker has developed as a corollary to his work, seems logically an independent and essential activity. The person who has complete knowledge of community resources need not combine any technique of treatment with his function of dispensing information concerning these resources. He should use the social case worker just as he uses the physician, the lawyer, the teacher, the government official in working out a situation.

Should this consultant upon community resources be necessarily a social worker? As social workers have been the persons in the community who have gathered all available data about social resources, have used and developed these resources more fully than any other group, have advised clients and representatives of every profession as to existing possibilities of service, it seems natural for the consultant upon community resources to be identified with social work. Where there is marked differentiation of social work, as in some of the larger cities, recognition of this specific rôle of consultant has already led to the establishment of information bureaus, either as a part of a welfare agency or as a separate organization. The New York Welfare Council is now seeking to amalgamate such services within New York agencies, since the advantages of centralization in dispensing information have been clearly demonstrated.

The suggestion that giving information be regarded as an essential activity of social work, does not imply change in present practice except in point of emphasis. The supplying of accurate information and suggestions upon the use of community resources is held to be of equal importance with social case work, and therefore a prime rather than a subsidiary function of social workers. Public support should be rather easily secured for this particular aspect of social work. The complexity of social organization points to the need of dependable advice available to all citizens. The immediate, tangible benefits from a social inventory could be readily pictured. The results in the future should be the discovery of gaps in necessary social services, the evaluation of various services in the light of the total services offered by the community, and elimination of waste and overlapping. In time the essential character of the several divisions of social service might be revealed, so that there would be less delay and mishandling due to failure to allocate to the physician the problems that are his, to the court, to the school, to the social case worker, the cases which lie within their provinces.

An increasing number of persons in recent years have been made responsible for studying what social work should be, rather than in doing any particular kind of welfare work. The results are evidenced in the federations and councils of social agencies, in the community chests, in the research and investigation bureaus which have been set up. Social workers have become analytical and critical of their own methods of work.[10] Though case work may still be the most characteristic and central activity of social work, perhaps the future lies in the hands of those who are observing and trying to evaluate case work as one of the techniques of social adjustment.

[10] See Chap. II.

VII

THE SOCIAL WORKER

ENOUGH has been said about the present status of social work to furnish a background for some specific consideration of the personnel of social work, of educational preparation for social work, and of the relationship of social work to the social sciences. Each of these aspects is a factor in determining what the status of social work is, and at the same time is essentially a product of that status.

So important is the personnel factor in shaping social work that one writer has offered as his opinion: "Social work is whatever the social worker does."[1] As has been pointed out above, the field of social work is ever-enlarging, ever-changing in response to new concepts of possible usefulness. Where the sphere of activity is of such elasticity, the type of personnel is of prime importance in determining what is done and how it is done, but one proceeds in a circle if a definition of the social worker is attempted in terms dependent upon understanding social work. The same point is reached when social work is defined in terms of what the social worker does. Illustration and description are more useful than definitions. The terms "social work" and "social worker" are admittedly not specific. A certain group, working in a fairly limited field, has preempted

[1] Tufts, *Education and Training for Social Work.* p. 18.

a title which carries no definite connotation to the layman.[2] There has been discussion of the possible substitution of "socician" for "social worker," but no progress is reported in bringing the term into use. The difficulty is not really one of terminology, however. The lack of a common denominator in the character of activities embraced is much more nearly fundamental to the confused state of present thought.

Considering only the central group which is conceded to be engaged in social work, there is a wide range of activities covered. The Vocational Bureau of the American Association of Social Workers compiled the following list of occupational groups:

Administration and Organization
1. Councils and Federations
2. Public Welfare Administration

Case Work
1. Child Welfare
2. Family Welfare
3. Medical Social Service
4. Probation and Parole
5. Protective Work
6. Psychiatric Social Work
7. Visiting Teaching
8. Miscellaneous Case Work

[2] "An interesting experiment was carried out in the streets of Toledo, Ohio, by students of the University Department of Social Work, who asked 350 'men on the streets' what their conception of social work was, and if they believed in it. Only seventy-five gave a fairly clear description, suggesting that it had a constructive and organized nature; fifty-three were unwilling to hazard an opinion. Of the 350 interviewed, 196 believed it should be supported, though only four thought it prevented social evils." *The Survey*, LIII (Jan. 15, 1925).

Group Work
1. Boys' and Girls' Clubs
2. Immigrant Education
3. Recreation
4. Settlement and Community Centers

Industrial Work
1. Employment Service
2. Handicapped
3. Investigation
4. Personnel and Factory Welfare
5. Vocational Guidance

Institutional Administration
1. Children's Institutions
2. Other Institutions

Public Health and Hygiene
1. Health Education, including Social Hygiene, Mental Hygiene, etc.
2. Public Health Administration

Research and Training
1. Social Investigation
2. Social Research
3. Teaching Social Work

Social Propaganda

Specialists
1. Financial Secretary
2. Nutrition Worker
3. Psychologist
4. Publicity Secretary
5. Statistician

In this list there are activities listed to which social work cannot establish an absolute claim. The field of education may call those engaged in immigrant education, in recreational work, in vocational guidance, in the teaching of social work primarily educators. Employment work is often regarded as a specialization of industrial engineering. The greater part of the public health and mental hygiene program is carried on by physicians and nurses with social workers as assistants. Those activities listed under *Research and Training* and *Specialists* suggest that persons with specific training in other fields are being utilized in social work organizations, with activities based upon their previous training. This latter group does not qualify as social workers any more than a probation officer at court qualifies as a member of the legal profession. The three first-named divisions—*Administration and Organization, Case Work,* and *Group Work*—seem to embrace the activities characteristic of social work. A social worker, then, is a person engaged in some variety of case work with individuals, in group work which has a recreational, educational, or civic program, in administration or planning for a single organization or for a group of social agencies.

The social worker is further characterized as one who has elected social work as a vocation and receives a salary for doing it. This distinction definitely narrows the group under consideration, for there are many volunteers carrying on the characteristic activities of social work. The volunteer may be of great use when properly directed and is no negligible element in a social welfare program, but should be studied apart from the full-time professional. A different set of circumstances operates in bringing the professional into social work.

What kind of person is employed in social work as a professional? There are comparatively few data other than those contained in the Russell Sage Foundation Studies of 1922 and 1925. Since there is no accepted classification of social workers, and neither the Census[3] nor any other body has undertaken their enumeration, the Russell Sage Study of 1922, which presents certain characteristics of a representative number, supplies the only material for general conclusions. The Russell Sage Study gives data as to education prior to entering social work, experience in other fields than social work, length of years of experience in social work, salary levels, salaries as related to sex, to years of experience, to type of activity, to educational background, and to geographical situation. The number employed in different occupational groups also sheds light upon the question of which are leading activities in social work.

Only certain conclusions will here be drawn from the data collected. In the preceding chapter there was some discussion of the educational preparation of social workers. About 44 per cent of those studied (1,258) by the Russell Sage were found to be college graduates, while 14 per cent had had one year or more in a school of social work. It was concluded that college education could not be assumed for social workers and that those who were college graduates had not, necessarily, any common knowledge of the social sciences nor of any subjects bearing directly upon the problems of social work. Though a number of the welfare agencies in the larger cities of the United States are stipulating a

[3] Census of 1920 classifies religious, charity, and welfare workers with fortune tellers, healers, keepers of pleasure resorts, etc., as semi-professional.

college education for new employees, the staff as a whole does not often meet this condition.[4] The majority of the agencies do not require college graduation of those employed, though, usually, the agency states a belief in the value of both college and professional school education.

Specific training in social work is even rarer than college education among social workers. The fact should be taken into account that no training schools were open at the time when many social workers chose their vocation. The numbers entering social work annually at the present time with and without social work training would give a more significant basis for determining the valuation now placed by social workers upon specialized training. No reliable figures are available as to the number entering without social work training. However, the four hundred produced annually by the schools cannot supply more than one-fifth of the positions open in social work—if the conservative estimate of an annual turnover of ten per cent among 20,000 social workers is accepted. It is apparent that the majority of those entering social work have not yet accepted the idea that such training is essential. On the other hand, there is considerable evidence to show

[4] Study of 740 social workers in Philadelphia agencies showed: 60.1% had high school education or less; 42% did not finish high school; 6.2% had only grammar school education; 10% had completed courses in schools of social work. Deardorff, "Education of Social Workers," *Annals of the American Academy*, Sept., 1925.

In a study of 66 leading social agencies of Ohio it was shown that 23 had some staff workers with only grammar school education; 25 had staff workers with only high school education; 4 had none except college graduates. Eubank, "Toward Professional Social Work," *The Survey*, LV (Dec. 15, 1925).

that many who have had experience in social work feel the need of professional training and seek to supplement their experience with courses in schools of social work.[5]

Social workers have a negligible common background of any kind. Not only is there little to be assumed as to their educational preparation, but they enter social work with a variety of experience in other fields. The Russell Sage report shows that the social workers studied had previous experience as follows:

Teaching	30%	(Of 1228 men and women)
Business	21%	(Of 1228 men and women)
Nursing	9%	(Of 1007 women)
Ministry	8%	(Of 221 men)
Journalism	6%	(Of 221 men)
Law	6%	(Of 221 men)

About two-thirds of the group had had experience in another field before entering social work; a number of individuals had had experience in several other lines of work.

The number of years of experience in social work offers a way of appraising the social worker's stability of interest. The median number of years' employment is about four and a half.[6] Here, too, it would be interesting to know whether the great increase in social welfare activities in recent years explains the large number of persons with rather short experience. On the face of the data available, the social worker's reputation for restlessness and instability appears justified. As

[5] During the academic year 1926-27, more than one-half the students enrolled in the New York School of Social Work had already had some vocational experience.

[6] Russell Sage Study, 1922. (Unpublished.)

in teaching, the number of young women of marriage-able age entering social work may explain a large loss from the vocation during early years of experience.

When salary levels of social work are touched upon, a subject of great importance opens up. Fortunately, there are recent figures upon the salaries of a relatively large group of social workers. According to the 1925 Study of the Russell Sage Foundation, covering 2,100 persons in 129 organizations situated in 81 cities of the United States, the median annual salary of the social worker was $1,517. A comparison was made with the elementary school teachers in cities over 100,000, whose median salary in 1925 was found to be $1,844. The two groups were at about the same level in 1913, the advantage being slightly with the social workers until 1919. Not only have the salaries of social workers lagged since 1919 as compared with elementary school teachers, but as related to the cost of living it is shown that the purchasing power of the social worker has scarcely advanced since 1913. For a considerable period purchasing power fell steadily below the 1913 level; only since 1924 has there been recovery to the pre-war level. The absolute gain in salary within the past twelve years is not worthy of mention.

Not only is the median salary of social work small, but the range of salaries is narrow—especially for the women, who comprise ninety per cent of the field. The following tables bring out these points:

Number of Women	Salary Received	Number of Men	Salary Received
1........	$8,000	3........	$8,000 or over
1........	6,000	6........	7,000-8,000
22........	3,000-6,000	12........	6,000-7,000
29........	3,000	12........	5,000-6,000
105........	2,000-3,000	26........	4,000-5,000
97........	2,000	49........	3,000-4,000
564........	1,000-2,000	41........	2,000-3,000
69........	1,000	41........	1,250-2,000
15...under	1,000	—	
—		190	
903			

Median salaries in social work have been related to college education, school of social work education, and years of experience in social work. Social work education or college education seems to secure a slightly higher salary for the woman with less than five years experience. A partially completed course seems to achieve the same salary as the full course. No combination of social work education with college education materially affects the salary. In the group which has had from five to nine years' experience the same observation holds. In the ten to fourteen years' experience group, it is noticeable that full social work education counts a little more towards salary advance than the full college course. There are only 111 women in this group—12 per cent of those studied.

Of the men who have had under five years' experience, those who have had full college education start at a higher salary level than those with social work education. Those without either college or social work education receive decidedly less salary. In groups with greater length of experience, college graduation appears to count more than social work education in determination of salary. The figures are not complete, however; 36 men or 19 per cent of those studied had had ten to fourteen years experience. In general, the men show longer social work experience than the women.

With both men and women there is an increase in salary with increase in experience until the maximum is achieved after about twenty years. After this point there is a definite recession. As indicated above, a comparatively small number of cases furnish the basis for any statements concerning those with more than nine years' experience.[7]

Another type of observation is based upon the salaries of men and women according to the size of the city in which they work and the type of position held. The maximum salaries in social work are received by men holding executive positions in large cities. Women, similarly situated, receive salaries which are about 50 per cent less than the men's. Almost the same discrepancy between men's and women's salaries in executive positions obtains whether the city is of large, medium, or small size. In staff positions the men appear to have relatively less advantage over the women, but the small number of men so employed makes the comparison of small significance. The salary scale for both men and women in staff positions shows little change by size of city; the executive salary scale varies considerably according to the size of the city.

As to the concentration of social workers in cities,

[7] Russell Sage Study, 1922.

the numbers employed in various social work activities, the type and grade of position held, there are some interesting figures:

Size of City	Percentage of All Social Workers Employed
Over 300,000	60
100,000–300,000	20
Under 100,000	20
(Under 25,000 . . . . . 8%)	—
	100 [8]

Type of Work	Percentage Of Women	Percentage Of Men	Percentage Of Total
Social Case Work	65	41	60
Industrial Case Work . .	4	5	4
Health Work	10	11	11
Group	12	17	13
Institutional	2	7	2
Organization	5	15	7
Promotion and Reform	1	1	1
Research and Teaching	1	3	2
	100	100	100
Grade of Position			
Executive	26	57	31
Sub-executive	7	14	8
Supervisor	18	6	16
Staff	49	23	45
	100	100	100

Evidence is clearly furnished that social case work is the leading activity of the field. The predominance of women in this activity is also shown. Almost three-

[8] Estimate of all social workers in United States—21,000; 4 to 5 to each 17,000 in cities with population over 100,000. Hurlin, *Proceedings of National Conference of Social Work*, Cleveland, 1926.

fourths of the men in social work are in executive or
semi-executive positions, while two-thirds of the
women are on the staff or in supervisory positions.

As to salaries according to type of work done, research and training lead all other groups. For men, the
salary starts $1,500 ahead of any other group, for
women, $1,000 ahead. This lead is maintained to a
large extent throughout the range of groups by years
of experience. Organization is the next best paid
activity for both men and women; health and employment work are pretty even; group work leads case
work except in ten per cent of the cases.[9]

From the variety of statistical data furnished, it is
now possible to draw a kind of composite picture of the
social worker. Usually, the professional social worker
is a woman who has had between four and five years
experience in the field and is doing case work. She is
working in a city of over 300,000 population and is
receiving a salary of less than $1,800. She has had
experience in some other field before entering social
work but has not completed college nor a course in a
school of social work. The chances are three to one that
she will not rise to an executive position, forty to one
that her salary will never be over $3,000 annually,
and almost three to one that she will not remain in the
field for more than five years after entering it.

So much of the picture is suggested by the statistical
data of the Russell Sage Studies. Other details may be
filled in with less exactitude. There is a charge frequently made against social workers that they are
lacking in sense of group loyalty and unity of purpose;

[9] Russell Sage Study, 1922.

that their interests are narrow. Not only does the community fail to recognize the social worker when it sees him, but social workers fail to recognize each other! The tendency to form organizations based upon a specific activity in the field of social work and to be oblivious to other organizations based upon other specific activities is said to be detrimental to the development of a general program and professional spirit. Social workers often appear more interested in the technique of certain jobs than in programs for social welfare. The justification of this attitude may be that social workers are as inarticulate in explaining their individual jobs to each other as in explaining them to the general public. The finite mind falls back for comfort upon the actual situation which he knows; so the social worker appears to be an individualist.

Such a picture has its limitations, of course, but it puts something concrete in the place of the vague concept of the social worker which frequently prevails. With this picture in mind it is possible to discuss how social work is affected by the personnel factor and also why the type of person described has been drawn into social work.

The skepticism of the contributing public as to the expediency of permitting social workers to make and put into effect a program proposing fundamental changes in legislation, industry, and social institutions has been mentioned as a serious limitation upon any attack on fundamental conditions underlying social problems. This skepticism is not attributed entirely to lack of confidence in the judgment of social workers but partly to the fact that neither social workers nor any other group has drawn a comprehensive and practical program. In the absence of definite findings by social scientists or recommendations from legislators, industrial engineers or educators, the public shows reluctance in admitting that intricate problems of social adjustment can be handled by the social worker. Social workers, taken by and large, have larger responsibilities than similar education and experience would bring them in well-established professions. If case work is made up of the intricate intellectual processes described, it is being entrusted to many persons of inadequate education and experience.

As was pointed out earlier, the public expects the social worker to make his contribution to charity in the form of low-paid services. Little progress from this point of view was evident until the movement towards welfare federations and community chests led to recognition that organizing ability must be procured at the market price in the business world. With the coming of a few high-priced (relatively speaking) executives into the field of social work, a new point of view on salaries has been introduced. The attitude now growing within the vocation is that social work must compete with the other professions in offering salary and other inducements necessary to attract those who have ability to carry out the program efficiently. So far, the public has done little to make possible the realization of this idea.

It seems clearly a disadvantage to have so few men in the field; social work is already known as a feminized profession.[10] As the problems of society concern both

[10] See p. 105.

men and women, the weakness of having a markedly feminine approach is obvious. Yet men who plan to lead a normal family life will hardly choose a profession with such low prevailing salaries. The point is often made that the opportunities for a man with executive ability are as good as, or better than, those in other fields. The answer is that the opportunities are good because there are now so few men with those qualifications; the opportunities are not numerous.

Another serious result of low salaries in social work is that adequate educational preparation becomes impractical. The social agencies assert that a full college education and one or two years of specialized graduate work is the kind of preparation desirable for social work. In practice, they state that they are unable to hold up these standards because there are not applicants available with such background. It is not to be wondered at when the beginning salaries—from $75 (or less) to $125 a month, according to size of the agency and the city in which it is located—are known. The schools of social work have a struggle to present clinching arguments for a specialized education of one or two years, when the agencies evaluate such preparation by offering only an additional ten dollars a month over the usual beginning salary. That the schools have rather small registrations and are unable to supply the full needs of the agencies does not seem curious.

The factor of competition with other professions calling for specialized training is definitely felt by schools of social work. Figures have been given showing that elementary school teachers receive nearly 22 per cent more salary than do social workers. Graduate work is seldom required for elementary teachers and there is a reasonable assumption that many persons might weigh teaching with social work as a vocation. In entering the nursing field, the student is subsidized while receiving training. Business requires little formal preparation, and usually offers more materially than does social work.[11]

The matter of salaries is crucial to the development of social work. As long as the public does not give high rating to the services performed by the social worker and does not accept the idea that salaries must be on a competitive basis with vocations requiring prolonged educational preparation and high mental qualifications, social work will probably not draw the type of person who will command social esteem. An interpretation of social work to the public must probably precede any improvement in the salary situation. If the public fails to respond to the argument that notable results cannot be achieved before firm foundations have been laid, progress will be long delayed.

The point is here made that the type of worker found in the field is definitely explained by the attitude of the public towards social work. The attitude of the public is in turn determined by observing social workers as they are. The low salary scale, which has been fastened upon as a prime factor in limiting personnel selection, has a profound reaction upon educational preparation for social work, and educational preparation affects equally the quality of social work done and the public attitude towards social workers and their activities.

[11] See p. 120.

The circle must be broken, and the logical place for breaking it is to recognize the need of a flexible salary scale.

In concluding this chapter, it is asserted that the social worker is essentially the product of those who find fault with him. Because the prestige of social work is not as great as that of the established professions, because activities are not clearly defined and are of uncertain character, and because material rewards are decidedly meagre, there are a limited number of persons of high calibre attracted into the field. This fact does not alarm all who have the interests of social work at heart; those who believe the basis of work to be primarily spiritual are loath to put forward any inducements to the worldly inclined. They feel that social work may lose more than it will gain if it is to be appraised in terms of self-interest. Yet, with the broad ideas current as to the equal value of many types of service, and with the modified rôle now assigned self-sacrifice in the good life, it is doubtful if social work can obtain the workers it needs without offering tangible rewards. Teaching and the ministry are both facing these hard facts; social work will probably follow in line.

VIII

PRESENT EDUCATIONAL FACILITIES AND NEEDS

IF social work is to supplement other vocations having a social aspect and is to draw together all the necessary elements of an integrated social program, a specialized education must provide social workers with a sound background. Careful preparation is essential for those who are to qualify for the specialized rôle of counselor on community resources. Furthermore, if social workers are to be placed in a position which permits a more confident appeal to the public for recognition of the value of social service, the adequacy of their training and qualifications must be clearly demonstrated. Upon what principles may an effective educational program be drawn?

Several studies of educational facilities and needs in the field of social work have appeared within the past five or six years. Professor Jesse F. Steiner in *Education for Social Work* presented a survey of the history of education for this field, of the origin of the leading schools, of the trend towards schools within universities, of the development of the curriculum, of the proper basis of education for social work. He analyzed the technical courses of instruction and raised several pertinent questions as to the relationship of social work to the social sciences, and as to practical standards of admission and achievement for training schools.

Two years later, in 1923, Professor James H. Tufts published a more comprehensive work, *Education and Training for Social Work*,[1] which analyzed the field of social work as well as the problems of education and training. This volume, which discusses in detail the questions of purpose, of personnel, of techniques, of financing, of supplementary education, of specialization in social work in the practical field as well as in the schools, has become the handbook of those interested in social work from a vocational point of view. The philosophy of social work, its relation to other fields of work, the obligations to be met in training and education, the academic environment suited to schools of social work, the level, graduate or undergraduate, upon which instruction is given—these and a variety of other topics are given consideration in Professor Tufts' book.

A third book dealing specifically with training for social work is Miss Elizabeth Macadam's *Equipment of the Social Worker*. Whereas Professor Tufts and Professor Steiner discussed the topic primarily from the standpoint of American conditions and practices, Miss Macadam emphasizes developments in Great Britain. She offers an interesting comparison between the British and American points of view. Miss Macadam visited the leading schools of the United States, the Canadian and European schools as well and, therefore, discusses points of difference and likeness with a broad perspective. The early university affiliation of training courses for social workers in Great Britain, as compared with the development of independent

[1] See Bibliography.

schools fostered by the social agencies in America, seems, to large degree, explanatory of the divergences in both philosophy and practice between the two countries today.

While these writings have been of help in clarifying the problems of education for social work by stating the nature of that problem, they have not succeeded in pointing a simple, direct way to the solution thereof. The situation is, unfortunately, a difficult one. Present education for social work continues to be far from satisfactory. The difficulties and complexities of the practical field result in confused demands for educational preparation. A field of work where activities are not clearly defined or classified, are ever-changing, are related to activities in a dozen other fields, and are of intricate intellectual nature, presents almost insoluble problems to the educator. Two choices are open to those who undertake the task: the first is to prepare workers for a limited set of activities for which some kind of job analysis can be made and in which opportunities for employment exist; the second is to educate, not for the vocational demands now manifest, but to develop workers capable of molding social work, who may, in some remote future, succeed in making social work realize its full potentialities.

The majority of educators for social work have apparently decided to prepare workers for tasks which can be fairly well described and which are commonly held essential activities. What form of educational preparation is proposed to meet the needs of such activities? Two types of preparation are advocated: one type is training on the job—apprenticeship—and the other, educational discipline in an academic institution. Only within the past ten years has there been any strength of numbers in the group backing academic preparation. Though schools of social work had a beginning in the United States as early as 1898,[2] the first full-time school of distinctly academic character was established in Boston in 1904 by Simmons College and Harvard University. By 1910, there were schools in the five largest cities of the country: New York, Chicago, Boston, Philadelphia, and St. Louis. Within the ten years, 1916-1926, twenty-five schools were established. There are now thirty-five schools in the United States and Canada having organized curricula in social work for full-time students.

The recent growth of academic training indicates that the period is brief during which men and women with this preparation could have influenced the field of social work. The majority of those in social work know nothing except apprenticeship training; therefore, their support of one or another kind of training may be rather blind. Some, who claim to have made an honest comparison of the two methods assert that education on the job—if there is proper supervision and the standards of work are high—is the most effective way to develop an efficient social worker. Others are willing to compromise by dividing the responsibility of the students' training with a school; that is, the school may conduct certain courses relevant to social work, and the social agencies may supervise the practical work to which the student usually gives at

[2] The Charity Organization Society of New York then established courses and organized what later became the New York School of Social Work.

least one-third of his time. The early schools of social work were often established upon the initiative of social agencies which felt the need of supplementing the practical experience of new workers.

The prevalent method of induction into social work is apprenticeship. What does this imply as to educational preparation? Nothing of uniform standard, surely. In some of the larger city agencies a definite number of apprentices is in training each year, with supervisors of known teaching ability in charge, and with definite standards of performance to be met before the apprenticeship period is passed. In other agencies the newcomers struggle along as best they may with supervisory authority centered in no member of the staff. After an indefinite period of time, they either acquire ability by the hit-or-miss method to handle their jobs, or become discouraged and leave. This is a wasteful process for all concerned, yet it is often encountered.

The majority of agencies fall between those which have a systematic training program and those which have none. Provision may be made for adequate training, but numerous "accidents" or "emergencies" necessitate breaking in upon the orderly schedule planned. Often the executives are themselves critical of their training methods but proclaim themselves impotent to change the situation. The argument of lack of funds, which counters every criticism of personnel and service standards, is usually raised. Trustees and directors are often unwilling to allocate salaries for supervision of apprentices and will not pay salaries over a period of time to those in training. Their lack of appreciation of what social work is attempting prevents the proper financing of apprenticeship training, just as it prevents the establishment of a generally satisfactory salary scale which would permit the alternative of academic preparation.

The chief reason for apprenticeship training is economic, as revealed by the data on salaries. Many social workers, however, heartily endorse the apprenticeship method and point to the records of those who have been taken straight from college to prove that there is no superiority in specialized school training. They may overlook the fact that the agencies are giving the schools little opportunity to show what they can do. Many of the larger city agencies recruit directly from the senior classes of women's colleges, offering training and salary from the moment of entry to those whom they feel best qualified for social work. On such terms social work may make an effective appeal to the girl who is eager to get into "the midst of things." The result may be, as is often stated, that the agencies skim off the cream and that those who come to schools of social work for graduate courses are of less initiative and outstanding ability. Little evidence exists that the agencies are, on principle, urging specialized education and giving salary recognition for it. The agencies appear alert in realizing all that is possible from the initial advantage of offering the college graduate a job without asking further educational preparation. If the agency acts with the idea of filling immediate staff needs and believes that it is impossible to command specialized educational preparation under the present salary scale, the policy is short-sighted. If there is sincere conviction that the apprenticeship method of training has merit, a fair testing of this method should be planned. The future of social work depends upon a square facing of the problem of what educational preparation is necessary to establish adequate standards; joint effort upon the part of schools and agencies will be requisite to insure the achievement of such standards.

Undoubtedly, those who support apprenticeship training in principle have been forced upon the defensive in late years. They have been led to recognize that their attitude is not calculated to help the case of social work as a profession, and that there is great weight to the argument for specialized training if social work is to command that respect which is necessary for effective operations. Retreat is in order to the next position—that is, that the practical problem of raising the salary scale sufficiently to make possible the requirement of specialized education, is well-nigh insoluble. Unfortunately, no definite data exist to prove that agencies lose or gain by employing as they do. Turnover figures do not lend themselves to easy interpretation, and there is little in the nature of production records. The fact, mentioned earlier, that those receiving service are not given the opportunity to express their judgment in the selection of their advisers—as would be the procedure if they were paying for service—precludes the most simple test of the social worker's success. In the professions, there is such an objective rating given by the client; business lends itself to tangible measurement of performance; social work alone seems to be entrusted with the responsibility of appraising its own workers and works.

A second group—those who accept the field of social work as it is and believe that specific educational preparation should be provided—has gained ground at the expense of those advocating apprenticeship training. The backers of this position may, in fact, be said to hold the ascendancy at present among those actively interested in social work education. Inasmuch as the majority of the schools of social work were initiated by social agencies, members of the faculty, who have often had considerable personal experience in social work, reflect an acute consciousness of the practical needs of the field. Not only because they are keenly aware of obligations to the agencies, but also because they feel that they owe it to their students to prepare them for actual openings, the schools usually build their courses upon existing demands.[3] Desire to show results in placing graduates advantageously is natural in this period when the schools are struggling for recognition. When the question is yet unsettled as to whether school training "pays," the schools try to produce some concrete proof to back their reasoning. This object may be best achieved by placing students in positions which have practical influence upon the field.

Accepting, then, the idea that their function is to prepare workers for existing situations in the field, how do the schools proceed? Naturally they seek to prepare for those divisions of the field which are of central importance and of definite enough character to be

---

[3] A statement was made by the Secretary of the New York School at the meeting of the Association of Schools of Professional Work at Chicago, Dec. 1925, that all courses were developed in view of the existing situations.

analyzed. They prepare case workers of all kinds, community organizers, visiting teachers, institutional workers, executives of social agencies, or give supplementary education to persons already holding such positions. A number of the schools conduct correlated courses for public health nurses. In general, they prepare upon the assumption that the students will go into agencies supported on private funds. Public welfare positions are, as yet, awarded chiefly on the political preferment basis, and little recognition is accorded educational preparation. It is generally believed that the standard of public welfare work is inferior to that of privately supported organizations. Consequently, students usually have their field work in private agencies, and their training is quite definitely restricted by this fact. The schools insist upon the practical point that there is no alternative choice, as so few public organizations do work of the standard which they wish students to accept. Furthermore, they hold that there are too few positions open in public welfare to justify specific provision.

The schools are preparing, therefore, for a decidedly limited range of social welfare positions. Not only is the concept of activities limited, but present educational preparation for these activities is not provided except when carried on under private agencies. Certain attempts are being made, especially in the state universities, to draw state welfare institutions into contact with private agencies and with the training school. In general, it appears that the schools have done little specifically to narrow the gulf between private and public welfare work. In the South and in the West, the private agencies are not so deeply entrenched as in the North and East, and there are many more activities covered exclusively by the public agencies. The effect of this different situation is already reflected in educational methods and in the future will probably be even more noticeable. The schools in the East are older and have set certain precedents from which the newer Western schools are slow in breaking away. Following the logic of building upon the actual needs of the field, there is good reason, however, for variation from Eastern practices in the Western and Southern schools.

Another limitation of the older schools is their absorption with urban problems. The city creates many maladjustments and tends to bring out others which are overlooked in the country, but there is undoubtedly neglect by organized social work of acute rural situations. That only eight per cent of all social workers are employed in cities of under 25,000 must be interpreted as showing that a very unequal distribution is made upon the basis of existing social problems. Society's lethargy in facing new problems is the probable explanation of the inadequate attention now given rural sections where social problems undoubtedly exist. The American Red Cross made a definite effort to improve rural health and recreation facilities during 1919-1922 and gave an impetus to educational preparation for rural social work by financing certain courses in a number of Middle Western and Southern Universities.[4] Though the Red Cross public health work is still extensive, the support of training schools by direct

[4] Viz., Universities of North Carolina, Indiana, Missouri, Wisconsin, and Tulane University.

contributions has been discontinued. Scholarships for public health nurses are often supplied, but little is done to encourage students to prepare for other forms of rural social work.

The fact that schools of social work attack a limited field and confine their preparation of students to certain activities within that field would not be serious if preparation for other important social welfare activities were elsewhere provided. There is little doubt that much social welfare work now carried on by private agencies will at some future date be incorporated into municipal and state departments. The experience of a democracy in the development of educational and health programs points definitely in this direction. The leading reason for support of private organizations is that they may experiment without undue restraint, may develop fruitful lines of approach to social problems, and may set standards against which public enterprises may be checked. The transfer from private to public funds of enterprises which present legitimate claims for consistent and abiding support in the interests of society as a whole should be accomplished when feasible. Education of the public for the undertaking of new responsibilities, and education of personnel to hold the new positions created, would seem indispensable to the success of such a transfer. The schools of social work appear to be doing little to advance this cause—probably due to practical limitations already indicated.

It is true that much of the training in schools of social work is as good a preparation for public as for private welfare work and that some workers go over from private to public agencies. The increasing tendency to make appointments to important public welfare positions dependent upon Civil Service examinations rather than upon political preferment will undoubtedly stimulate educational preparation. Educators in the field of social work have as yet accomplished little in securing the adoption of satisfactory standards by those who give or grade the Civil Service examinations. It is admittedly difficult for the schools to educate in advance of the development of a public opinion as to minimum standards in public welfare work; there is, nevertheless, an opportunity for leadership by the schools.

Social workers can not expect to go far towards the goal they have set themselves without the coöperation of public welfare agencies. When their language, let alone their philosophy and ideals, is barely comprehensible to public officials who share their tasks of promoting social welfare, how far can they expect to get with a general social program? The entire police and penal system, the institutional care of dependents, delinquents, and defectives, the official handling of immigrants, housing and factory inspection, public recreation, and various other welfare activities are in the hands of those who have had scant or no educational preparation for the social aspects of their work. Other neglected fields from the standpoint of specific educational provision are adult education and public administration. Can the social case worker attempt single-handed to adjust the individual to social conditions, if so many other agencies with which the individual comes into contact fail to see the problem in a similar way? The job of these other agencies may be a quite different one from the social worker's, but their influence upon the individual may be as potent, and, unless there be common understanding, one may render the work of the other ineffective.

The scope and multiplicity of public welfare activities have been discussed in Chapter II. The desirability of having them intelligently and efficiently directed appears self-evident. The amount expended in the United States upon all public welfare activities would probably total a billion dollars annually. Though any estimate of totals is approximate, it is clearly evident that the ratio of public to private expenditures for welfare work is steadily rising. Many of those who are active in community chest movements state that the maximum of what can be raised from private sources may have been reached. The tactics of the community chest are said to be calculated to expedite a transfer of the financial burden to tax funds, since an attempt is made to secure contributions in proportion to the individual's resources, carefully ascertained. In a democracy there does not appear to be a great step between persuasion and assessment. When compulsion is felt to contribute to the community chest, the individual may not react very differently from when he pays taxes.

A responsible group must direct public welfare activities, not only because large sums of money are entrusted, but because the activities carried on touch the happiness and well-being of many individuals. Work of such nature calls for an intelligent, well-educated group, disinterested, and possessing initiative, with high qualifications as citizens. Preparation for such work should not be of fortuitous character; schools of social work would seem to be the logical place to expect provision for sound preparation.

According to the picture drawn, only a small area of social welfare work is now being served by schools of social work. Fostered by private social agencies, which embrace a limited range of activities, the schools have addressed themselves to preparation for three or four central vocations, carried on in urban regions by organizations supported through private philanthropy. If such preparation fits the student for a wider range of activities, this is rather by-the-way than the result of explicit planning. Not only the field work but the case records and other classroom materials are drawn from these private agencies, and the body of data at hand indicates that graduates from the schools are largely absorbed by these same agencies.

To return to the earlier statement that the leading idea today among educators for social welfare is to prepare to meet the existing demands of the field, analysis shows that "existing demands" has a concrete and restricted meaning. Those demands of the field which are sufficiently explicit to result in the setting of educational standards for workers and in the offering of salaries sufficient to make preparation feasible, are demands which the schools seek to meet. Little recognition is now given to needs which are not backed by effective economic demand.

What other attitude can the schools afford to take towards the needs of the field? One or two have broken away from the ranks and have undertaken to build a curriculum and to set objectives according to their ideas of how the field of social welfare might best be served. They are definitely in another camp from those which base their educational plans upon the effective demands of the field as now constituted; they subscribe to the faith that students should be turned out from the schools capable of directing social work along new lines and of breaking down undesirable present limitations upon the vocation. This is a daring attitude when there is so little certainty among social workers or in the academic world as to what the future program for social work should be. It is a faith in experiment and in a thoroughgoing attack upon the fundamental problems of social welfare, rather than assurance that there will be backing from the practitioners of social work or from the general public. The fact that the present status of social work and of schools preparing for social work is unsatisfactory on so many counts means, however, that no strategic ground is surrendered in taking up a new position. There seems every reason for taking an independent stand in the present situation. The schools may fulfill a double function in preparing students for positions in social welfare and, at the same time, in examining critically the ground which should be covered by social work.

A start has barely been made in the direction of establishing what constitutes satisfactory preparation for social work. Few of the schools have challenged the premise that they must meet the present demands of the field, though many of them recognize the restraints thus imposed upon the curriculum. The marked growth of schools within universities will undoubtedly expedite the establishment of changed criteria for the schools.

A re-evaluation of teaching methods and materials will gradually be made in terms of the general program of the universities. Where there is duplication or lack of coördination with courses given in other schools, adjustments will be made. Time and a frank acceptance of the school of social work as one of the divisions of the university will bring about needed standards as to adequate preparation.

In what has been said in the preceding paragraph, two things seem to be assumed: first, that there is sound academic ground upon which specialized education for social work may be built; and second, that the practical demands of the field can be met by putting preparation for social work upon this sound academic basis. The first assumption must be considered at length; the second is felt to hinge definitely upon the first, but is by no means automatically resolved at the same time. It is easy to foresee that there will be a struggle before executives of social agencies will be persuaded that a broad preparation for the general field of social welfare is more desirable than training for the specific jobs which are open in their organizations; that restlessness and desire to advance from one type of position, or from one type of activity to another should be encouraged among social workers; that the effectiveness of any social organization is of small moment as compared with the effectiveness of the social welfare program of a community—in other words, that they must renounce practically all their vested interests in training for social work.

IX

SCHOOLS OF SOCIAL WORK

THE thirty-five schools of social work now existing in the United States and Canada might be studied in a number of different ways. The first method would be to analyze each individual school. The history thus revealed would usually be interesting and distinctive, for a variety of local elements has molded each school. Training for social work is a large and uncharted educational undertaking, giving ample play for personalities and immediate situations to determine the character of a particular school. One school, for example, is found to emphasize preparation for medical social work, because it is situated near a hospital with a well-organized social service department offering advantages for field work, and because, furthermore, the director of the school has had considerable experience of this kind. A second school is found to stress the legal aspects of social welfare work and to present a number of courses in social legislation, thus reflecting the particular training of members of its faculty. It is generally true of academic institutions that the approach to subjects and the emphasis upon different aspects of these subjects are somewhat conditioned by the traditions of the institution, by non-academic factors such as location, amount of endowment, and, above all, by the personalities of the teaching staff. The individual history of schools of social work would reveal these elements to marked degree.

A second method of study would be to assemble some comparative data upon the schools as to plan of organization, academic standards of admission and graduation, size of budgets, number of faculty, number of students, number and type of courses given, departmental divisions, scholarships offered, amount of tuition, placement and subsequent records of students, titles of theses presented, etc.

A third method would be to examine the activities of the Association of Schools of Professional Social Work, which includes two-thirds of all the schools and has, to some degree, built up a group concept concerning objectives of social work education. The semiannual meetings of the Association with their systematic programs may offer a clearer idea of trends in social work education and the philosophy that is being evolved than can be obtained by studying individual schools, which are as yet unable to tear themselves from local situations that delay the fulfillment of desired objectives.

The first, or case-history, method hardly seems practicable for present purposes, as interest centers more upon the status of social work education in general than as to what any particular school is achieving. Where an individual school illustrates certain tendencies, it may be useful to establish its identity. As a rule, the second method of study, based on comparative data, seems more profitable and will be chiefly used. The generalizations which can be drawn as to actual status of the schools should serve as a substantial background for the third method of study—analysis of Association programs and addresses—which will be attempted to a limited degree.

A survey of the organization of the thirty-five schools indicates a distinct trend towards linking up with a university. Of the thirty-five only five are entirely independent of a university. In the case of these five— the New York School of Social Work, the Pennsylvania School of Social and Health Work (Philadelphia), the Training School for Jewish Social Work (New York), the Atlanta School of Social Work, and the National Catholic Service School (Washington)—each has definite arrangements with a local university by which some faculty and courses are provided for the school. Of the remaining thirty schools, fifteen are organized as separate schools within a university, six are classified as separate departments, and nine are organized within a university department, usually the Sociology or the Economics Department.

As to admission requirements, eleven schools are upon a graduate basis, though nine of these accept some alternative to graduation from a full college course. Fourteen universities provide both undergraduate and graduate courses, the majority of the students being in the undergraduate courses. The remaining ten schools are on a distinctly undergraduate basis. The trend towards graduate status is not so marked as that towards inclusion within the university, though the opinion is expressed among educators for social work everywhere that a graduate course is preferable. In the next breath, however, there is an exposition of the difficulties in the way of achieving graduate status. These difficulties are largely the same mentioned earlier as interfering with any academic training for social work—that is, the low salaries prevailing in the field and the failure of social agencies to discriminate in favor of professional training when setting beginning salaries. Those who support undergraduate training usually agree that it is not as satisfactory as a graduate course, but state that it is possible to combine some professional work profitably with a liberal arts course. As teaching, which seems more nearly comparable to social work in required qualifications than any other vocation, demands usually no graduate work, certain educators believe it necessary to develop undergraduate preparation for social work as a matter of expediency.

Though many admit that graduate work of the right kind would present many advantages over undergraduate preparation, some maintain stoutly that undergraduate training may accomplish all that present graduate schools are accomplishing. Their argument may be summarized as follows:

1. A coherent course may be planned through four years, preparing for social work and fulfilling all requirements for the B.A. degree.

   The student begins to concentrate upon the social sciences in the sophomore year.

   In the junior year some specific technical courses in social work are given and also some practical field work.

2. Prevailing salaries in the field for social work do not justify the average student's taking graduate work. The median salary of staff workers (except executives) of social organizations in cities over 100,000 was $1,157 in 1925, the median salary of elementary school teachers, $1,844.[1] Median salary of secretaries

[1] Russell Sage Study, 1925. (Unpublished.)

in 1925 was $1,638.[2] Neither of these latter groups is required to have graduate work.

The following objections are advanced to undergraduate training:

1. Students in the undergraduate college are too immature to handle the subject matter of social work.

   The material is too complex for their comprehension.

   It is unfair to bring young persons into contact with the almost insoluble problems of the persons with whom social work deals.

2. Social work involves assimilation of a body of material too large in quantity to be superimposed upon a liberal arts course.

   Vocational courses interfere with the necessary foundation courses. Field work can not be fitted into the schedule of the undergraduate students without sacrificing college courses or the social agencies' interests.

The most important point at issue seems to be whether or not the subject matter of social work can be effectively handled in the undergraduate college. Some survey of the subject matter to be covered is needed before forming an opinion. There must be consideration, first, of the subject matter now included in schools of social work and, second, of the possible modifications in curricula which might affect the feasibility of undergraduate preparation.

There is no obvious classification of courses within the thirty-five schools studied, since there is no accepted terminology. As far as possible, the purpose for which a particular course is designed has determined its grouping in the following list. The relative importance

[2] Bureau of Vocational Information, Secretarial Study, 1927. (Unpublished.)

of the subject, as indicated by the number of courses given in these thirty-five schools, is represented roughly by the order in which given.

1. Social Case Work . . . .
{
Family Case Work
Child Case Work
Psychiatric Case Work
Hospital Case Work
}

2. Community Organization
{
Group Work
Recreation
}

3. Medical Social Work . . . .
{
Psychiatric Social Work
Public Health Nursing
Hygiene
}

4. Care of Delinquents and Defectives
5. Social Research and Investigation
6. Publicity and Administration
7. Personnel and Industrial Service
8. Child Welfare

Social Philosophy, Social Reform, Psychology, Sociology, Social Legislation, Economics are always represented by a course or two and, as a group, include more courses than any other.

As the list stands, it presents quite a technical aspect—certainly the titles of courses are not those usually found in the arts college curriculum. It is necessary, however, tó inquire as to what their content is. The most important body of courses deals with some aspect of case work. In an earlier chapter[3] case work, as the central activity of social work, was discussed in some detail. The demand for systematic preparation of the case worker in schools of social work rests upon belief that procedure can be generalized, though little is claimed as to transmittable technique. The social

[3] See chap. V.

worker is evolving treatment gradually out of experience and observations, as the physician did in the past, but is handicapped by having small opportunity to measure results or to supplement clinical observations through laboratory research. What the student in a school of social work is expected to acquire is a scientific attitude towards observation and collection of data, ability to analyze and plan upon the basis of all pertinent facts. In the class room and through field work the student also gains a knowledge of community resources, skill in assembling them with respect to various types of cases, ability to diagnose the client's disability, and constructive imagination in getting results. The social worker's procedure is said to be made up of a combination of acts "which no untrained person, however intelligent, would have achieved."[4] The method in the schools is class-room discussion of prepared cases, of student experiences, combined with responsibility for the actual handling of a certain number of cases.

Upon examination, other technical courses in the curriculum are found to involve an application of social case technique to various fields. For instance, personnel and industrial service as taught in schools of social work are based to considerable extent on case work. So also are the courses in community organization, group work, child welfare, recreation, the care of defectives and delinquents. Underlying all of these subjects there is a unifying principle which is social case work. The schools often proclaim this fact by making courses in the principles of case work introductory to

[4] Richmond, *What is Social Case Work?* p. 102.

almost every division of the field, and by requiring half a year's field experience in a family case working agency before the student is allowed to specialize.

In the majority of the other courses listed in the schools there is little technical material. Statistics, sociology, labor problems, health and hygiene, social legislation, psychology, publicity, and social administration contain material familiar to students in the undergraduate colleges and professional schools. In schools of social work these subjects are doubtless presented from a certain angle and with a specific purpose in mind, but the general content is not novel.

From the point of view of the disposition of the student's time, field work is the most important part of the professional school's requirements. Usually two full days a week under careful supervision are required, and frequently even more time is given. For the majority of the schools this has been the most difficult part of the program to arrange, as it involves the coöperation of a number of local agencies. There has been a ceaseless struggle to see that the student's work in the agency is really educational and that individual interest is not subordinated to the smooth functioning of the agency. In some instances, the school pays part of the salary of an agency staff member to insure real supervision of its students. Recently in certain schools it has been so arranged that designated faculty members of the school act as staff members of social organizations. In such cases, a definite district may be assigned for student training.[5] As the conditions of field work

[5] Both the New York School and the Chicago School have adopted this plan.

become more controlled by the school, academic credit is usually given for field work.

The first point to be considered in determining whether instruction in social work can well be undergraduate turns, then, upon the question of the possibility of handling case work courses satisfactorily. According to the Director of the New York School of Social Work, there are two objectives in social work instruction.

1. Acquisition of working concepts and knowledge regarding field objectives, etc., of social work.
2. Development of student's native abilities to put into practice this body of knowledge.[6]

In a somewhat detailed explanation as to how these objectives are achieved, it is strikingly apparent that actual contact with the field is all-important. Technique is acquired through field work alone but must be coupled with classroom work. A great deal is said about the necessity of high personal qualifications, some of which may be developed in the course of the school training.

All of which, when summed up, means that the student learns by doing, and the school provides opportunity for development of native skills under supervision. If this is really what case work means, the argument that the subject matter is too complex for the undergraduate mind falls to the ground. The argument centers about whether the students as undergraduates can bring sufficient maturity to the subject and whether the training can be fitted into the schedule.

[6] Lee, Address before Association of Schools of Professional Social Work, December, 1925.

In regard to the second point—the question of maturity—one falls back upon general opinion rather than any body of fact on which a conclusion can be based. Obviously, the undergraduate student is younger than the graduate student and presumably has had less contact with life. The problems which the graduate student meets in social work are less apt to disturb his balance if he is himself an adjusted person. Relying upon the assumption that a completed college course and a certain number of years in the world have brought this adjustment about, the graduate student has an advantage in entering social work. On the other hand, there is nothing to prove that it would not be possible to develop the student by varied experience with social problems throughout the whole undergraduate course, so that by his Senior year he would be better adapted to social work than is the graduate student whose previous experience has been fortuitous. If, for other reasons, it is thought desirable to provide under-graduate education in social work, the matter of maturity does not seem an insurmountable obstacle.

The third point which has to do with the difficulty of fitting education for social work into the undergraduate schedule seems a very important practical one. Since preparation for social work relies upon social case work and purposive field work continues to be the backbone of such courses, there is considerable objection to introducing it into the liberal arts college. The interest both of the student and the agency requires that the field work should be of substance and not some minor clerical job. If any real responsibility is given to the student, it is more than likely that he will have to ignore certain formal classroom regulations. Furthermore, the agencies in which the students do field work must be physically situated near the university. Many of our state universities are at some distance from any large city and the opportunities for field work are thereby limited.

If education for social work is to continue to center around the acquisition of the technique of case work, it does not seem feasible to include such training in an undergraduate course. One alternative has been worked out in a few places where the student is given considerable background work before graduation and then has a year of interneship in a social agency, remaining more or less under the supervision of the university.[7] Another alternative would be to place less emphasis upon case work. Many critics of the present system feel that the emphasis upon case work in practically all American schools is due to the long period during which training for social work was under the dominance of the social agencies and has no justification in principle. In Great Britain, where the schools at a much earlier point in their history became associated with universities, there is not the same tendency to put case work in a central position. The emphasis is upon social philosophy and a general course of study "to develop the right attitude of mind toward future work." British social workers apparently have little sympathy with the American emphasis upon case work and insistence upon vocational courses.[8]

Furthermore, it may be said that although the

[7] The University of Wisconsin operates under such a plan.
[8] Macadam, *Equipment of the Social Worker.* pp. 58-190.

majority of the schools give much attention to the acquisition of technique, their efforts meet with small approbation from the agencies. Everywhere there is the complaint that the schools' graduates do not really fit into the working organization of the agencies and have to begin at very much the same point where non-graduates begin. It is admitted that often the school graduates move ahead faster because of their superior background, but little is conceded as to their immediate usefulness.

In summary, therefore, it may be said that the argument that the essential subject matter of schools of social work is not fitted for undergraduate instruction is inconclusive and can be combatted at every point. That is, it is believed that there is little material presented in the schools which is too complex for under-graduate comprehension; that it is possible to prepare young persons psychologically for social work through purposive direction of experience; that, with the exception of courses in case work, the greater part of the subject matter is borrowed from courses already in the liberal arts curriculum; and that the difficulty of teaching case work with its necessary corollary field work can perhaps be legitimately met by placing less emphasis here.

The conclusion drawn from this discussion is that no complete demonstration has been made of either the adequacy or inadequacy of undergraduate instruction for social work. Many factors, productive of incon-clusive results, complicate the situation in both under-graduate and graduate schools, making comparisons or evaluations unprofitable. If there is essential soundness in the argument that salaries in social work cannot be sufficiently high to justify graduate preparation for the majority of those entering the field, the development of an undergraduate curriculum which will cover some of the desired ground seems necessary. An alternative sometimes suggested is provision of fellowships and scholarships for graduate study, or payment of partial salaries for students' field work by the agencies. There are obvious disadvantages in following the road which the ministry and teaching have traveled in becoming subsidized professions. The immediate gain which might result from offering fellowships to promising students must be weighed against the possibly unfavorable reaction upon the general salary level. A sound salary policy is a prerequisite to satisfactory status for social work; its achievement depends upon realization by the public that social work is important; that persons of high ability must be drawn into it; and that the compensation must be sufficient to hold them. If preparation for social work is subsidized through fellowships, the psychological effect may be that social workers are considered under an obligation to repay through service what has been advanced. So, the justification of low salaries would continue, though the religious or self-sacrifice motive, which was stressed in an earlier time as proper for the social worker, may have been somewhat transformed.

The practice of paying students for their field work also has inherent drawbacks. The agency which pays the salary either looks upon this as a scholarship which will insure the student's later acceptance of a staff position in that agency, or believes it possible to obtain full value from the student's services at the time rendered. In both instances there is danger that the individual's educational interests may be jeopardized. Furthermore, any such arrangement usually results in the student's doing most of his field work in one agency. Such limitation of experience appears a handicap if it is assumed that field work will provide the student with varied experience and a basis for choosing the special line of work in which he is interested. The only effective argument for allowing the student to receive a partial salary from the agency is that the immediate practical problem of financing the student's training is solved. Quite conceivably he will find later that he has paid dearly for the respite by helping to keep down the general salary level in social work.

Underlying most of the discussion which takes place as to what educational preparation is desirable for social work is the assumption that all persons entering the field need the same general type of training. The schools of social work often state explicitly that they seek to prepare students of first-rate calibre for positions of leadership. Considering the great need for leadership, the schools appear to have exactly the right idea. But if preparation for social work is eventually to be a necessity for all entering the field, it may be well to raise the question whether preparation is to be the same for every one. A good deal is said about the minimum qualifications requisite for any type of social work and a comparison is drawn with the medical profession. The analogy is not a telling one, however, for, though the training for medicine is long and of exacting nature, there is a distinct trend in the direction of making the courses of study largely elective and of a length which takes account of the use that the individual is planning to make of his training.[9] The idea is becoming firmly established that individuals cannot afford to spend time and money on training which they will not use.

In social work there are many types of positions, calling for a wide range of personal qualifications and specialized training. In reading much that is written one might suppose that all occupational divisions in this field were vertical rather than horizontal. The suggestion is offered that social work may be comprised of many "planes," calling for as varied and definite grades of preparation as are represented in the field of medicine. A laboratory assistant does important work for which he must be trained, but surely his education is not to be that of the surgeon. Similarly, the preliminary interviewer in a welfare agency requires some background, but not that of the man who runs a community chest. Much of the confusion which exists in the field of social work has previously been attributed to lack of analysis and classification of jobs. When the actual work of the field is determined, educational objectives can be more easily set. It seems likely that, in view of the practical demands of the field, preparation for social welfare work will range from specialization in vocational courses given in the undergraduate liberal arts college to a graduate course of several years in a professional school.

[9] "We have seen that it is impossible to set aside any definite set of facts or skills as constituting the 'best' training for medicine. Medicine is scientific, if at all, mainly because of an attitude, and technique, with certain obvious exceptions, the particular facts learned, the particular skills acquired, are of less importance than the habit of inquiry, the ability to use the sense, the capacity for well-directed effort." Flexner, *Medical Education*.

Looking at the actual situation, one finds that little enthusiasm for backing undergraduate courses in social work can be aroused. The courses now operating have too often been set up in rather haphazard way to meet the demands, only half-comprehended, of local social organizations or of students. The curriculum resulting may be made a part of the Sociology or Economics Department, and may not have the whole-hearted backing of any member of the faculty. A department head has been known to establish a curriculum not through any real interest in social work, but rather to prevent a separate school from growing up in the university.

The university's lack of confidence in social work may be stated positively as applying to both graduate and undergraduate courses. In only a few cases can the school, department, or curriculum of social work be said to have won an established position in the university and to be regarded as a legitimate university activity. There is often real antagonism displayed when social work is not established within one of the recognized departments. The reasons for this distrust are probably numerous—opposition to the inclusion of vocational training in the liberal arts college; lack of belief in the need of special preparation for social work; lack of confidence in social workers, due to low standards still prevalent in the field; lack of sympathy with the objectives of social work; feeling that the qualifications and skill necessary for social work should be acquired on the job rather than at the university; belief that the courses given are shoddy and attract inferior students.

The result of all this belief and feeling is that there is usually very little coöperation in adapting courses already in the university to the needs of the social work group. When analyzed, many of the under- graduate courses in social work show only a sequence which may or may not provide real education for social work. There may be two or three courses in the principles of case work and provision for some field work, more or less adequately supervised—altogether offering little support for an opinion that the under- graduate course might be satisfactory. In a few places where there has been sincere interest in developing an undergraduate course and some experi- ment with it, the tendency is to swing over to the graduate course, or, rather, to introduce an additional graduate year after the undergraduate course. Many members of school faculties feel that the undergraduate years must provide an integrated general preparation for social work, which will become a necessary pre- liminary to the graduate year's work; they are not willing to say that the undergraduate work provides adequate preparation in itself. How much of this dissatisfaction with undergraduate preparation is due to the difficulty of fitting field work into the program it is impossible to say. Certainly, there is more said about the limitations of undergraduate preparation in this respect than in any other.

The Association of Schools of Professional Social Work has not come to any conclusion upon the relative value of graduate and undergraduate preparation. The basis for membership in the Association was stated as follows in the Constitution adopted June, 1919:

Any educational institution, maintaining a full-time course of training for professional social work covering at least one academic year and including a substantial amount of both class instruction and of supervised field-work may become a member of the Association upon election by the Executive Committee.

There has been no formal modification of these basic standards, but a statement made in the fall of 1924 by the Executive Committee gives some detailed suggestion as to fundamental principles which should be recognized in establishing a course in professional social work. The main points covered are:

A. That there should be "an organic grouping of relevant courses of instruction into a special curriculum for the stated purpose of vocational or professional education for social work."

B. That these courses should consist of:

1. Background of pre-professional courses.

2. Specific knowledge courses to be given by specialists in good standing outside the field of social work.

3. Technical knowledge courses to be given by one or more social workers eligible for senior membership in the American Association of Social Workers[10] with adequate academic qualifications for teaching.

[10] The membership standards of the A. A. S. W. are as follows: There are two kinds of individual membership in the Association—Members and Junior Members. Qualifications for Membership comprise four years of practical experience in social organizations of a recognized standing, and an educational equipment and background, which, combined with the experience, seem to give promise of sound professional achievement. For Junior Membership, one year of practical experience and graduation from an accredited college or university are requisites.

    4. Technical training courses to provide skill, consisting chiefly of intensive field work under supervision of well qualified social workers who are salaried and voting members of the faculty of the school.

C. That there should be a director as the executive head of the school empowered to exercise control over admission requirements and general standards.

D. That the coöperation of allied professions and the resources of hospital, dispensary, court, school and other social agencies are necessary to develop adequate training for social work.

The latitude permitted in these very general statements as to standards has been fully exercised by the twenty-five members of the Association. Ten of the schools are organized on a graduate basis, eleven offer both graduate and undergraduate preparation, four are entirely undergraduate.

As there is difference in academic standards of admission, there is wide disparity in length of courses, requirements for degrees or diplomas, size of faculty, number of students, departmental specializations, amount of tuition, attitude towards securing employment for graduates, etc. Professional preparation, if graduate, seldom comprises more than a full academic year. A master's degree rather than a diploma is usually awarded, and, in such cases, the academic requirements concerning a thesis must be met by the graduate students in social work. In several schools the regular course is six quarters (two academic years), except for those who have entered with extensive background in the social sciences or with practical

experience. It is important to note that while the requirements for degrees and diplomas may be strictly
upheld, the majority of the students in the schools never
fulfill these requirements. Students enter without fully
meeting the academic standards of admission, they
study for a semester or a year, and leave without
completing the course.

In the undergraduate university courses there are
seldom any professional or technical courses before
junior year. Field work may begin in the junior year
but does not often absorb much of the student's time
until senior year. The junior student may have only
three hours of field work weekly; the senior may carry
as much as nine hours. Considerable difference is
found among schools as to the kind of field work
approved and as to methods of supervision and instruction of students in field work. Dependence upon
social organizations to provide facilities involves
delicate questions of policy. The agency must feel an
obligation to consider the student's interest and to
insure that his work is of educational nature; at the
same time, the agency must be run primarily to fulfill a
purpose which is quite outside student training. In a
limited number of places, the two interests involved
have been satisfactorily reconciled.

The schools show marked divergence in number of
faculty and students. Often, it is not a simple matter to
decide what the number of faculty is. Where the
curriculum is set up in a university, there may be no
one teaching social work who is not also teaching
courses in some department of the liberal arts college.
Or the great majority of the faculty of a school, especially

of a school organized outside a university, may be made up of officers of local social agencies giving part time to instruction in the school. The schools often make large use of lecturers, who may be borrowed from the university, from other professions, or from the social welfare organizations. A list of all those who instruct in a given school may give a quite erroneous idea of size. On the other hand, the list limited to full-time faculty is apt to be lacking in significance, as it is only natural for the school to borrow in the way above described to insure breadth of view and for economy's sake. Enumerating faculty on the basis of those whose chief obligation appears to be to the social work curriculum, the highest number is thirty-six as recorded by the New York School of Social Work, and the lowest, two, in the University of Wisconsin.

In discussing definite data relative to the schools, there seems some justification for choosing a few which are important from the standpoint of number of students or of contributions to educational experiment, rather than attempting to generalize about all thirty-five schools. From a study of the New York School of Social Work, the School of Social Service Administration of the University of Chicago, the School of Social Work of Simmons College, the Smith College School for Social Work, the Pennsylvania School of Social and Health Work, the Bryn Mawr Department of Social Economy and Research, the School of Applied Social Sciences of Western Reserve University, the School of Public Welfare of the University of North Carolina, the curriculum in social work, largely under-graduate, at one of the Middle-Western universities such as the University of Minnesota, the University of Wisconsin, the University of Michigan, or Ohio State University, a rather complete picture of what is significant in social work education may be obtained. These schools are contributing over half the total of trained students and are the leaders in methodical experiment.

Of this group only the New York School faculty has over ten members whose central interest is teaching courses in social work. Seven or eight is the usual number upon the faculty of a university school. About one-third of the faculty have the degree of Ph.D. More than half hold a degree higher than a bachelor's degree; one in ten holds no degree. The field work supervision and teaching of case work is often in the hands of a person holding only the bachelor's degree; occasionally he may have a master's degree.

As to publication, the faculties of schools of social work are more given to producing for current periodicals than to writing textbooks or books upon the general subject of social work. Such magazine articles deal almost uniformly with "current problems," or with the methods and techniques of social work. They appear in a limited number of journals more or less devoted to the interests of the field.[11] At the University of Chicago a definite program has been undertaken to compile teaching materials for use in schools of social work. One or two volumes of source material are being produced annually. In general, it may be said that the faculties of the schools are notably unproductive from the publication standpoint.

[11] See Bibliography.

The non-academic activities of the faculty are numerous and diverse. Due to the fact that many enter into the teaching of social work after extensive practical experience, the staff of the school of social work is looked upon as an advisory body in community undertakings. The social organizations draw upon the school for members of their boards and committees; they count upon obtaining general leadership and coöperation from the schools. The citation of the number of committees or boards upon which faculty members serve may not convey much idea of the importance of these activities, but it is revealing. Four and a half typewritten pages are needed for enumeration of the outside activities of one member of the New York School—activities including membership on local and national committees, projects and surveys carried on, addresses made, membership in professional organizations, and publications. In this case there is perhaps a more complete record than in others, but the indications are that faculty members of schools in the larger cities quite often serve on ten or twelve committees interested in public welfare, give a dozen or so addresses within the year, attend several conferences, and maintain informal relationships as consultants to a large number of local organizations. They are active community members and their influence is by no means to be measured entirely in terms of academic activities. These relationships are exceedingly valuable both to the school and to the community. The school is vitalized and maintains the realistic approach which is essential for the accomplishment of its purposes; the community profits by the disinterested and objective point of view of the school faculty.

The effect of the close contact of the school with its immediate environment is seen in the research projects carried on by students. Where theses are required, the emphasis upon practical pieces of investigation is marked. Adopting the two classifications of (1) works of scholarship, covering studies made upon library material and upon data already amassed, and (2) works of practical investigation, where the student himself assembles material upon which his thesis is based, the schools of social work are seen to be holding themselves to concrete tasks. The division is about 32 per cent of these of the first type, and 68 per cent of first-hand investigations and experiment.[12]

Certain data in regard to the student body can be gathered as a basis for generalizations. As in the case of the faculty of the schools, it is difficult to say exactly how the student body should be classified. The total enrollment of the New York School in 1925-1926 was 475. Of this number 319 were classified as pre-vocational, 45 as vocational, 4 as non-matriculated, and 107 as extension students. In June, 1926, 27 diplomas were awarded to those completing the course. In addition, there were over two hundred students in the Summer School and Institutes. At the School of Social Service Administration of the University of Chicago, the total registration in 1925-1926 was 412. Of these, 133 were classified as graduate students, 62 as undergraduates, and 217 as extension students. During the academic

[12] A few titles of theses at the University of Chicago in 1925-26 may illustrate the kind of study made: "Housing Conditions in the Stockyard District," "Street Trades," "Tenement House Ownership among Immigrant Workingmen," "A Study of 466 Delinquent Girls with Institutional Experience."

year 1925-1926, the Ph.B. degree was awarded seven, the M.A. to twelve, and the Ph.D. to two.

In the universities conducting undergraduate courses, it is practically impossible to obtain definite figures as to students preparing for social work, since they are usually grouped with those specializing in the Department of Sociology. If the university gives no certificate in social work, there is nothing to indicate how many receiving degrees are prepared to enter social work. Add to this the fact that the schools or departments seldom have adequate clerical facilities for record-keeping, and the difficulty of estimating what number of students is under the school's influence becomes evident. Certainly, the number of graduates from the course gives a very incomplete picture of the work of the school. It is of great interest to note that while only a small number of those enrolled take the full professional course, there are large numbers coming into the school for supplementary education who put its teachings directly into effect as they resume their practical work. In the New York School, where over half of the students in regular courses and almost all of the Extension and Institute students have had previous experience in practical social work, a central purpose seems to be achieved in vitalizing and broadening the social worker on the job, rather than in preparing students to enter social work.

Another way to indicate the importance of schools of social work would be to study the subsequent records of those graduating. The lack of adequate record-keeping on the part of the schools as a whole makes any generalizations as to careers of graduates out of the question. Several of the schools have almost complete records and some conclusions may be drawn which apply to the graduates of those schools. For example, the Smith College School for Social Work states that median salary and turnover for their graduates are very different from the average shown in the Russell Sage Studies of 1922 and 1925. The New York School claims that of 250 graduates from its full course only 10 have changed their field of work. Those schools which have records show that their graduates are in positions of strategic influence in the field of social work. It is uncertain how much credit the schools can claim for their graduates' subsequent success, since many of their students have made fair progress in the practical field before they attend the school. The data are too inconclusive and incomplete to permit definite statement as to the advantages secured by school graduation.

It is apparent, however, that the schools make a good point of entry into the field of social work, since a majority furnish a formal or informal placement service for students and assume considerable responsibility for placing graduates advantageously. The local agencies always look to the schools as one source of supply; national organizations apply regularly to certain schools. In fact, the schools complain constantly that the agencies make it difficult for them to hold on to their students, as positions are offered during the period of instruction. The tendency for graduates to take positions within close physical range of the school is marked.[13] Certain schools, however, are drawing

[13] Perhaps this is due somewhat to the fact that the school was originally selected because it was near the student's home or center of interests.

students from all parts of America and from Europe and distributing them as widely.

Alumni associations and occasional bulletins are other methods, in addition to placement service, for keeping the schools in touch with their graduates. The placement bureau appears to be the most definite and, in a number of cases, the only tie. Information is usually forthcoming from the graduates only when a new position is desired and, therefore, is irregular.

Data as to tuition and expenses of the school courses, fellowships, and scholarships offered, and budgets of the schools would seem to be, of necessity, of definite nature. Tuition is of varying amounts in the schools mentioned as significant in the development of education for social work. In the state university schools and departments the tuition is usually that prevailing elsewhere in the university, which means that state residents may pay no tuition. In the Middle Western universities tuition, even for non-residents, is seldom more than $125 per year; at Western Reserve, $250 per year. Additional expenses are very difficult to estimate but vary according to cost of living in the city in which the school is situated.

Data on scholarships and fellowships are much less simple to assemble than tuition data, since here again there is often no distinction made between students of social work and students majoring in Sociology or Economics, as the fellowships are available to all graduate students. It is evident, however, that certain schools have felt that the most feasible way to recruit desirable students for social work is to offer financial inducements. The Bryn Mawr School of Social Economy and Social Research, the New York School of Social Work, and the Smith College School for Social Work have a number of fellowships which cover a considerable part of the student's necessary expenses. The state universities seldom have much to offer except general graduate fellowships in the university. At the School of Applied Social Sciences of Western Reserve University, at Johns Hopkins University, and at the Pennsylvania School of Social and Health Work, an arrangement by which the student receives a salary from a local agency in which field work is done may be regarded as an alternative to offering fellowships to attract desirable students.

Study of the budgets of the schools furnishes little enlightenment. The figures for schools in the universities are somewhat buried in those of the general department within which they are usually administered. Further, there is seldom any attempt to estimate what the university contributes in supplying overhead expenses, nor is there recognition of the money value of supplementary university courses in which students of social work may register. That the school within the university may be conducted at much less expense than the independent school is clearly evident. A comparison of the budgets of the New York School and the University of Chicago School illustrates this point, as the budget of the former is practically five times that of the latter (1926-1927). Charging up a reasonable sum for general overhead expenses, there is still a very large saving at the Chicago School, which is to be attributed to the School's ability to draw upon other schools and departments of the University for integral parts of its curriculum.

Another conclusion that may be made after study of the budgets is that, in general, they are very scant. Salary levels for the faculty reflect the low standards of the field; lack of clerical help, of libraries, of adequate quarters, and of research facilities results in small budgets but at a great cost in effectiveness of program. There is little to draw men of superior ability to the faculties of these schools when facilities for work are not more adequate. In a number of places only a crusading spirit and sincere belief in the program can account for the personal sacrifices that have been made by those promoting education for social work. Acceptance of large responsibilities, overwork, and infinite worry do not necessarily lead to the advancement of a successful program. Lack of leisure may explain to large degree the failure of school faculties to produce publications, and their failure to orient themselves in the general field of the social sciences.

The third method of studying education for social work through the Association of Schools of Professional Social Work does not turn up much new material. The fact that such an organization exists and with the avowed intention of raising social work to professional status is interesting. It was a distinct step forward when the schools of social work were willing to modify their strongly individualistic proclivities to the extent of joining in an association designed to develop group standards of training. As was earlier pointed out, the Association has done little so far to achieve standards of admission or graduation which have value, and membership does not yet imply common objectives or methods. The influence exercised by the Association is of rather informal, indirect nature. At the time of application for membership a school is subjected to some scrutiny and questioning by the Executive Committee. Once admitted, there is no machinery for checking up on the work of the school. There are no paid officers of the Association, no business office, no funds for travel or investigation, no publications; so any direction given an individual school is of personal and advisory nature.

The Association convenes twice a year for a session of several days. At Christmas it meets in connection with the annual conferences of the national societies of the social sciences; in early summer, with the National Conference of Social Work. At both times business meetings are held and there are daily sessions open to those interested. Papers are read and discussed at the open meetings; an excellent opportunity is afforded for the schools to learn what each is doing. Furthermore, a philosophy and policy as to education for social work is being developed in these group meetings. Joint sessions with the American Association of Social Workers are also valuable in bringing together those who share the responsibility of trying to elevate existing standards of social work. Discussion is frank and concrete upon points raised as to policy and practices. Still, there is a consciousness throughout the group that no real authority is vested in it. There is provision for free discussion, but little action. Committees are appointed and return reports containing recommendations, but not much is done to put such recommendations into effect.

Unless the Association establishes definite standards of membership and sees to their enforcement, there seems small reason for excluding any schools which are interested in becoming members. The value of membership now lies not in the prestige of having met certain requirements, but in the exchange of opinion and in the stimulation which comes from contact with those facing similar situations. Surely, the schools which are lagging behind the majority should have the benefits of such contact. The Association probably would accomplish nothing by the adoption of hard and fast standards of membership; enforcement of such rules would be both impossible and injudicious. No staff of any existing school is so confident of its present organization as to recommend a general duplication of its set-up. In fact, among those responsible for the schools there is a note of deprecation, almost of apology, in appraising what has been accomplished in light of the task still remaining. Hence, there is now no basis for setting absolute conditions of membership, though the attainment of certain minimum standards of membership is a desirable goal.

What the Association may accomplish at the present time is to keep the isolated schools in touch with the field of education for social work as a whole, to prevent the repetition of recognized mistakes, and to accelerate developments of wholesome nature. This service cannot be rendered in a spirit of coercion but must create its own demand. If the service is as valuable as it should be, it will soon be sought with eagerness, for many of the schools admit to perplexity and discouragement in attacking their problems.

Furthermore, the Association should be able to voice the opinion of the schools in meeting with the American Association of Social Workers, and with the national associations of social organizations, which wield considerable influence in determining professional standards and salaries. The schools cannot proceed far in realizing professional status unless they have the coöperation and backing of others in the field. A program backed by the schools would have great possibilities of uniting many now seeking responsible leadership. Such a program can be evolved out of the present Association of Schools of Professional Social Work.

X

SOCIAL WORK AND THE
SOCIAL SCIENCES

PROBABLY the independent development of social
work and of the social sciences explains to a large
extent the gap in thinking between those who promote
social welfare and those who study the phenomena of
social behavior. Social work has passed through many
stages of development, each characterized by different
objectives and a different philosophy. The period at
which the social group first recognized the need of
charity towards weaker members antedates history
itself. The motives for charity have undergone steady
change and its forms have altered with the evolution of
social and industrial life. During the Middle Ages in
Europe, the church became the source and sponsor for
humanitarian activities. The gradual shift of responsibility to civic and non-religious groups has even today
been only partially accomplished. As previously pointed
out, a large amount of philanthropic work is undertaken with the idea of fulfilling a religious duty,
thereby storing up personal grace and helping to
elevate the soul.[1]

With the Industrial Revolution, some of the employing class assumed certain responsibilities for the
personal welfare of employees. The paternalistic motive,
coupled with a business interest, gave impetus to many

[1] See chap. I.

philanthropies and much legislation.[2] Also, increasing
wealth, growth of cities, and improved means of communication gradually produced a sense of responsibility in society at large towards the problems and
sufferings of the poor. Further growth of industry
brought in its wake an impersonal atmosphere, due to
size of plant, corporate ownership, etc., and, in con-
sequence, the necessity of activity by the community in
directing and supplying relief to many outside the
sphere of either church or employer. Disinterested
citizens organized to secure both public and private
funds for the relief of the distressed. Labor unions
sought to insure the individual rights of their members
through group action. Both the state and employers
were put under pressure to provide for the illness and
destitution of industrial workers. Today the state
shows a tendency to take to itself responsibility for
maintaining those services which appear to be per-
manently needed for the promotion of social welfare;
private philanthropy still must point the way in meeting new situations.

During the greater part of its history, social work
has been chiefly concerned with relief—finding some
remedy for immediate ills. At the same time there
has been an ever rising standard of relief and an
attempt to carry those in distress over the crisis and on
to solid ground. Meeting the situation adequately
means a study of causes for distress, which, in turn, has
led to interest in prevention. Today, appeals to the
public and educational campaigns for social welfare
programs make large use of the word "prevention."

[2] Queen, *Social Work in the Light of History*. See chap. IV.

And along with this appeal, not as yet emphasized to the same degree but insistent, is coupled a new term—"constructive work."[3] Naturally, there is no conflict implicit in these three approaches—remedial, preventive, constructive—but the character of social work largely depends upon which purpose is dominant. When social work seriously applies itself to the study of prevention of existing ills and seeks to arrive at a program of social welfare based on positive, constructive principles, the basis for an affiliation with the social sciences will have been laid.

The development of the social sciences has been markedly different from that of social work. Each of them has an origin far back in the past, but as sciences with the epithet "social" affixed, they are of recent date. Economics, for instance, as a science dealing with material wealth was studied by the Greeks and developed as a distinct body of thought in both England and Germany during the fifteenth, sixteenth, and seventeenth centuries. Not until the eighteenth century was "social economics," which studied the economic surroundings of man, his motives, and his activities in the production of wealth, recognized in the writings of the Physiocrats and of Adam Smith as an integral part of economics. Today the use of the epithet "pure" to designate that division of economics which expresses the problems of value and exchange by mathematical formulas suggests the interest which economists have found in developing the theory of their science. Present study and interest center, however, upon the economic problems of contemporary life, with consideration

[3] *Ibid.*, chap. III.

of human behavior as an important factor in those problems.

In psychology the influence, first of philosophy and ethics, later of biology and physiology, has, until very recently, led to emphasis upon man as a moral and physiological, rather than as a social, being. Contributions towards the understanding of normal man in his social relationships have been slight. It is interesting to note that sociologists rather than psychologists frequently teach social psychology in universities. Also, some of the most important discoveries for psychology have come through psycho-pathologists who are of the medical profession.

The chief field of historical interest has naturally lain in the past, with little specific interest in the immediate problems of modern civilization. Recently, historians have acted more fully upon their knowledge that all the world is not at the same stage of development, that certain facts learned from experience may be checked against present social phenomena, and that the trend of events may be marked at the time of occurrence.

Anthropology has contributed knowledge as to man's physical and racial history, has supplied a vivid picture of past societies, has indicated racial interrelationships, and has made valuable studies of living primitive groups. The light shed upon present-day problems is mainly derived from these sources; the focus is seldom directly upon such problems. It is patent that the complexity of civilized life makes studies of existing society immensely difficult as compared with studies of past and primitive societies.

Political scientists have a long record through past centuries of studying the responsibilities, the forms and extent of civil government, and the resulting effects upon public and private affairs, but emphasis appears often to have been upon the legal and material interests of the state and the individual, rather than upon total social relationships.

With the advent of sociology as a new science dealing with all the phenomena of human society, supposedly a synthesis was effected of the social aspects of the various sciences. Perhaps it is too soon to say that sociology has failed to accomplish this; at the present time, it is still floundering somewhat in its attempt to find stable ground which can be held as its own. Certainly few would go so far as to say that the study of sociology supplies all the knowledge of social phenomena which concerns one seeking to understand human behavior. Sociology has undoubtedly taken over territory unclaimed by the other sciences and of great significance.[4] Knowledge of these other sciences seems, however, complementary. While there is no question that the primary aim in sociology is an understanding of social relationships, the criticism directed against this study is not on the score of any lack of interest in social problems, but of lack of effective contributions to these problems. Sociology is charged with spending its energies in seeking status by the development of the paraphernalia of a science rather than by shedding light on social problems. The tendency to vocabularize

[4] "Indeed it may be said that sociology has become the first attempt to organize a technique for scientific interpretation of human experience upon the basis of the group hypothesis in contrast with the individual hypothesis." Small, *Origins of Sociology*, p. 346.

has been mentioned; many charges seem to boil down to resentment against what is felt to be unnecessary complication of simple facts.

The sociologists are not discouraged with the showing they have made. They claim to have turned other social scientists in the direction of self-analysis and of interest in actual problems of social life.[5] In short, they feel the credit is theirs for the recent realistic trend in university social science departments. Also, much of the progress in treatment of social ills is held to emanate from the findings of sociology. It is stated that since sociology developed, social treatment has improved immeasurably.[6] Whether or not there is a positive correlation between such progress and the contributions of sociology, which is not dependent upon other factors of time and general social conditions, has not been demonstrated. At least, the sociologists are admittedly interested in problems of treatment and seek contacts with those handling social problems.

Out of this short outline of the history of social work and of the various social sciences, a few conclusions may be drawn. During the past there was little reason for social work and the sciences to know of each other's work and program, for they had little in common. Only recently has there been a basis of mutual interests; social work, on the one hand, has developed an explicit interest in prevention and, therefore, in causes; on the other hand, the sciences have become realistic and desirous of studying problems of human behavior at

[5] *Ibid.*, chap. XIX.
[6] Blackmar, "The Sociology Complex" in *Journal of Applied Sociology*, III (January-February 1926), 203-212.

first-hand. Unlike the approved way of building a tunnel where the two groups start to dig in expectation of ultimately coming together, social workers and social scientists have worked independently from two ends and have unexpectedly found themselves occupying adjacent territory. The query arises: Do they recognize their proximity and do they accept the fact that they must work out a program of development and expansion together?

At several points in the foregoing chapters, mention has been made of the relationship existing between social work and the social sciences. The dependence of the curricula of schools of social work upon standard courses in the social sciences was noted. Something was said, too, of the difficulty of obtaining recognition for technical courses in social work in the university, because they seem to be at once closely related to those offered in sociology and economics, and yet widely different. Earlier, in the discussion of social work as seen by the social worker,[7] the claim was considered that social work is scientific because it makes practical use of principles drawn from the social sciences, applied in accordance with a carefully developed technique. Further, the assertion was noted that, in developing this technique, the social worker, through observation, collection, and analysis of social data, made a valuable contribution to social science, when, and if, procedure was well-ordered and duly recorded.

Apparently, then, there is recognition on the part of social workers that they *should* draw upon the social sciences. They feel rather than act upon this idea. In

[7] See chap. VI.

spite of general statements that social workers must be well-grounded in psychology, sociology, political science, economics, in order to succeed in their difficult tasks of social adjustment, it is patent from a study of those in the field that they are not so equipped. Furthermore, in schools of social work—which presumably give to a few the desired kind of education that is denied the majority—the admission requirements as to prerequisites in social science are seldom at all comprehensive, and even more seldom are those in existence enforced. Those courses in social science which are part of the schools' curricula frequently seek to provide knowledge of general principles rather than to interpret principles already acquired in terms of the specific interests of social work. Evidence points to little real appreciation by social workers of the connection between their work and the findings of the social sciences.[8] Lip service is often given, but with no definite idea of benefit now derived or of that which might be derived.

Not all social workers fall into this group which concedes respect and admiration but has little understanding of what the social scientists represent.[9] Sometimes real antagonism is expressed. It is said that social science purposely keeps itself in a realm which permits little practical testing of its findings; that the academic world prefers to view social problems from a distance or when conditions are properly "controlled." This means, says the social worker, that few vital contacts

[8] See footnote, p. 103.
[9] Bruno, "Understanding Human Nature," *The Family*, VIII (April, 1927), 58 ff.

with pressing problems will be made. Therefore, the abstractions and guaranteed statements which the social scientist permits himself are of little practical use to those who want advice upon particular problems. It is against the sociologist that discontent is likely to flare up, since the sociologist appears to deal in the theories most apt to yield some crumbs to the social worker.[10] The criticism directed upon sociology is that it is content to attach a name to a problem, generalize about it, and then pass it up. The social worker who eagerly awaits suggestions to be developed into a technique of treatment finds this very unpalatable.[11] The easy-going type, who is willing to develop a technique without reference to scientific precepts, finds his justification in the failure of the sociologist to meet the actual situation.

What is back of this mixed attitude of hope and disillusionment, which characterizes the attitude of the social worker towards the social sciences? Have contributions been as numerous and as valuable as they might have been? Is the root of the difficulty lack of practical objectives—and, therefore, from the point of

[10] A recent inquiry by Prof. T. D. Eliot of the Sociology Department at Northwestern University among many of the leading and older social workers of the country definitely brought out that they are not conscious that sociology has anything specific to offer them. See Eliot, "Sociology as a Prevocational Subject: The Verdict of Sixty Social Workers," *American Journal of Sociology*, XXIX, 744.

[11] "The social worker who reads the sociological literature and who sees great promise and hope for a more scientific type of social work in the sociological point of view, finds himself in the condition of the thirsty wanderer in the desert who sees a mirage and expects to drink his fill only to be bitterly disappointed at the frustration of his hopes." Karpf, "Relation between Sociology and Social Work," in *Journal of Social Forces*, III (March, 1925), 419-427.

view of the social worker, lack of achievement—among the social scientists? Are the channels of communication between social work and social science inadequate? Or are social workers assuming that the scientists should undertake a rôle which is not really theirs? It is necessary at this juncture to see how the social scientists view their obligations and general relationships to social work.

A marked difference in point of view distinguishes the approach of the scientist to the problems of social welfare as compared with that of the social worker. The former is interested in analyzing existing situations, finding out how they have come about, experimenting as to possible variations which may be effected by introducing new elements or by making new combinations of elements. He disavows any responsibility for saying what are desirable developments in social and economic life; he refuses to discuss or evaluate human behavior or social situations from the standpoint of ethics. The social scientist looks to the philosopher and to the statesman to indicate how social life and individual behavior are to be directed. His idea of the legitimate sphere of social work activity is putting through a practical program with objectives suggested by the philosopher and the statesman and with techniques contributed by the social sciences. He admits his own responsibility in discovering the methods by which desired objectives can be achieved and recognizes the need of reducing these methods to techniques applicable by the social worker to practical situations.

The social worker, on the other hand, is apt to assign a different rôle both to himself and to the scientist.

He draws no clear distinction between the functions to be exercised by himself, by the philosopher and statesman, by the social scientist. Sometimes he appears to assume the rôle of the philosopher himself and to be ready to state the objectives of a social program. At other times he appears to look to the social scientist for leadership in the drawing of a welfare program. At still other times—and it is in these instances that he brings severe criticism upon his head—he seems to overlook the need of having definite objectives. This willingness to proceed without a clear idea of end in view and to make use of techniques which are not of scientific origin are practices which scientists deplore in social work.

The social worker is interested in human beings as such and deplores the aloofness of the scientist from emergent social situations. He apparently feels convinced that science holds the key to the problems of human behavior and tries to stir the scientist to action by seeking to arouse his sympathies and sense of responsibility. The scientist resolutely declines leadership in promoting welfare programs and is profoundly skeptical of assertions made by social workers that their techniques are founded upon scientific findings. The scientist is well aware of the relatively small amount of scientific data which is capable of conversion into practical technique.

It is easy to understand why the social worker and the scientist are distrustful of each other when there is such divergence in point of view as to what the obligations of each are in questions of social welfare. Perhaps the social scientist has gone too far in insisting that

benefiting individuals and promoting social welfare
are no concern of his. He cannot be unaware of conditions which press in upon him in his daily life, and,
other things being equal, there seems a good argument
for selecting his problems for study from among those
which are of critical nature, socially considered. And
perhaps there could be more interest in interpreting the
findings of science into form which is usable by the
social worker. While social scientists have been wise in
improving and testing their methods before attempting
to take a realistic interest in social activities, they may
now be too reticent in pushing experiment and in
making use of the tools they have forged.

The social worker will not enlist support until he
accepts the scientist's own estimate of the rôle which
science is to play in furthering social welfare. He must
not approach the scientist as a promoter and a propagandist but as technician seeking counsel. Objectives
must be clearly stated and responsibility for choice of
objectives must not be imputed to the scientist. The
social worker must, furthermore, develop an attitude
and skill which will enable him to put into practice the
data which science furnishes.

Social scientists maintain that little of practical social
work is based upon scientific data. They are surprised
by the prophecy that social work may become an asset
to social science, at the same time that social science
becomes directly contributory to social work. A few
social workers and a few sociologists who stand on
border territory have asserted that social work has a
real contribution to make to social science. This point

of view[12] is rather new and apparently not taken seriously —if known—by many social scientists. Even if asserted stoutly, it would need considerable backing in facts to command credence. Yet a good case might be made if the potentialities of social work rather than its present weaknesses are examined, for the strength of social work, as well as its weakness, lies in its close-up view of real situations. The contacts with existing social problems are first-hand and vital. If science could order and control the data concerning society which flow to the social service organizations, a most valuable source of research material would be provided. Furthermore, the recognition of an authentic interest by science in the assembling of such material should prove beneficial both to social work and to social science.

What is needed to bring about this desirable end? Probably most important would be confidence on the part of the scientists that social work is touching significant human situations. Then, there would need to be belief that social workers could be trained to collect data of value and in a form suited to use by the scientist—which might mean that the social scientist would see reason for interesting himself in the training of social workers.

As to the likelihood of the social scientists' recognizing that what is done in the name of social work is, or is not, of concern to them, the attitude of the public insures that there will be increasing pressure exerted to force participation in shaping welfare programs. Draw-

[12] "It is one of the puzzles of the development of social case work that it has grown independently of any theoretical discipline, although all along its pathway it has been bordered upon or it has trailed a number of strange gods." Bruno, "Understanding Human Nature," *The Family*, VIII (April, 1927), 58.

ing a precedent from the contributions made to industry by the physical sciences, society, now conscious of problems of pressing importance, turns to the social sciences with the expectation of receiving aid.[13] The demand from the public for tangible contributions has already become a factor in social science research and has led to the strengthening of social science departments in the leading universities of the country and to participation in practical affairs by members of the social science faculty.

Social science is not permitted to develop in an isolated sphere unobserved by the layman. That so much of the material of the social scientist is of the fabric of everyday life—so familiar as to interfere often with perspective—is a real source of danger. Popular literature, the newspapers, advertising attest the superficial absorption of the vocabulary of the social scientists by the reading public. Such interest may indicate little intelligent understanding but does suggest a real need of leadership. Among statesmen, philosophers, and educators, there has developed an explicit belief that further mechanical progress endangers civilization because the physical sciences have progressed so far beyond our knowledge and control of social phenomena.[14] Many of this thoughtful group look to the social sciences for relief from the situation.

[13] Randall, *The Making of the Modern Mind.* See chaps. XXI and XXII.

[14] "With the allegiance of our age and generation so completely committed to the natural sciences, we must face the fact that the social mechanism can be kept from cracking under the strain only as we develop the sciences that relate to man. Unless we can marshal behind such studies as economics, political science and sociology the same enthusiasm, the same approach and something of the same technique that characterize our treatment of physics and chemistry; unless the results of this research can

Undoubtedly, the pressure exerted from without has brought about changes in the social science departments of the universities. Increasing attention is given to social science as a whole, and the trend in both research and instruction is markedly realistic. The fruits of this change appear good, not only because tangible benefits accrue to society, but because it is being demonstrated that the social sciences are coming alive; that the most promising laboratory for experiment and observation turns out to be those very concrete situations which are troubling the statesmen, philosophers, educators, social workers, and others. Students with a new concept of the social sciences are asking for additional courses which will provide tools for handling concrete social problems. Whereas ten, or even five years ago, the undergraduate student specialized in economics, political science, psychology, with the idea of teaching a theoretical subject of rather abstruse, difficult content, many are now studying with the idea of fitting themselves for the handling of practical problems of non-academic life.[15] Courses in the liberal arts college of the university have been modified both as to content and emphasis. Furthermore, schools of business have borrowed from the liberal arts college whatever they

be applied to human life as freely and boldly as we apply the natural sciences to modify our methods of living; unless we can free ourselves of prejudice and stale custom and harness intelligence to the task of straightening out the relations of man with his fellow-men and promoting an intercourse of harmony and fairness—unless, in brief, in our generation we can make some appreciable progress toward this goal of social control, then pessimism has the better of the argument . . . ." Fosdick, *The Old Savage in the New Civilization*, p. 7. Address at Colgate University, June 22, 1925.

[15] "It will be discovered one day that the chief value of social science, far from being academic, is moral." Giddings, *Scientific Study of Human Society*. p. 38.

could find which promised to be of use to the business man.[16] Students of economics and psychology have found it not only interesting but profitable to interpret subject matter to the business world in terms which can be understood and applied.

Graduate work and research in the universities are yielding somewhat more slowly to the pressure of practical affairs and of insistent social problems. Nor can it be said that there is entire sympathy within the faculty of the university for the rapid development of practical courses in schools of business and in other vocational curricula. The new point of view has not penetrated without encountering obstacles. Academic aloofness and tradition are negative factors which usually inhibit any attempt to bring the outside world into closer contact with the university. And in the case of the social sciences there is recognized a particular hazard in mingling with the current rather than standing on the banks of the stream. The current is so swift and strong that he who wishes to observe and test needs a stout dependable craft under him. The social scientist may not, like the physical scientist, try out his boat on a quiet pond before venturing upon the stream. Few experiments of the same value as those carried

[16] A comparison of the 1916 announcements of courses of the University of Chicago and of Columbia University with the 1926 announcements as to courses in the social sciences indicates definitely: (1) the absolute growth in total number of courses given; (2) the modification of the technical nature of the curriculum of the School of Business by the introduction of general courses from the Psychology, Economics, and Political Science Departments of the liberal arts college; (3) the absorption into the social science departments of the liberal arts college of much of the material formerly regarded as proper to the School of Business; and (4) a great increase in the offerings in the social sciences through the Extension Department and the Summer Session.

on in physics and chemistry laboratories can be set up by the social scientist within the university. So, when he ventures out into the community, he does not simply extend his tested knowledge to a wider area. He undertakes a new function for which he is not entirely fortified by past experience.

Using the community as a laboratory presents problems of considerable difficulty to the social scientist. In testing theories relative to individuals in groups there are inherent complexities which challenge ingenuity and require a subtle technique. Some methods have been established as sound for limited application. Those who have led in studying group phenomena are, to large extent, relying upon quantitative data collected and interpreted according to the rules of the physical and exact sciences. A certain area of human activity can undoubtedly be studied to great advantage by such methods. But the social scientist is being asked to do more than observe social activities and state results. He is asked why people behave as they do and what can be done to make them behave differently, if change appears desirable. The behavioristic concept presented by recent psychologists gives firmer ground for experiment than has formerly existed.[17] Experiment must still

[17] "In speaking of experimentation, I do not forget the difficulty of making experiments in the social sciences. That difficulty seems to me almost insuperable, so long as we hold to the old conceptions of human nature. But the behavioristic concept promises to diminish this handicap under which economics and its sister sciences have labored. For we can try experiments upon group behavior. Indeed, we are already trying such experiments. We have experimental schools, in which the physical and social environments of the children are made to vary, with the aim of studying the relations between the stimuli offered by the schools and the learning response. So, too, we experiment with different systems of remunerating labor, different forms of publicity, different organizations for distributing

face the problem of juggling with individual lives for the sake of establishing facts. How far this can be done with the understanding and consent of the community remains to be seen. Pioneering and an adventurous spirit in combination with a scientifically trained mind are at a premium.

Probably because of the difficulties found in the way of studying social phenomena at first-hand, scientists have been reluctant to turn from their books to active participation in practical affairs. Admittedly, many of their theories are generalizations upon abstractions— not comments to be taken literally concerning any living person at a given point of time and space. Students have been specifically warned not to attempt to apply these generalizations to everyday life. The chief contribution to the problems of the present lies, apparently, in giving a point of view or point of departure; in recording and interpreting past human activities a more definite work has been accomplished.

Social scientists would doubtless agree to the necessity of some one's solving social problems but would deny their own responsibility for undertaking any experiment, except for the primary purpose of collecting and testing data of scientific value. Where two ends may be combined—a study of scientific interest which offers also a remedy for existing social ill—well and good, but the social scientist must not be *obligated* to contribute to "welfare" programs. This negative attitude is frequently modified, however, by the practical

products, different price policies, different methods of supervising public utilities, and the like." Mitchell, "Quantitative Analysis in Economic Theory," in *American Economic Review*, XV (March, 1925), 8-9.

advantages secured in tying up a piece of research with a program of social welfare. The interests of the scientist and of social welfare may be harmonized to the advantage of both, since a large measure of public coöperation is necessary for the scientist engaged in social research, and society has an incentive for giving this coöperation when a serious social problem is being faced.

At least two sound reasons can be advanced for the belief that the general research program of the social sciences would profit by continuous and intimate contact with concrete social situations. First, a valuable impetus towards research should result from direct observation of social phenomena, if experience here parallels that of industry and of the natural sciences, where research has clearly been accelerated by contact with actual problems. Second, the social scientist cannot be indifferent to seeing his work bear fruit, his observations becoming the basis of new activities. Putting his facts to work should furnish both a check on their value and a stimulus for further research.

How is the desired rapprochement to be brought about between social scientists and social workers? They must come into contact with each other, learn to speak the same language, and develop mutual confidence.[18] The tendency for schools of social work to seek university affiliation suggests one means of bring-

[18] Within the year 1927, there were two developments which should provide valuable contacts: (1) The American Association of Social Workers was one of nine organizations asked to appoint a committee of three to assist in compiling the projected Encyclopedia of Social Science. (2) The American Sociological Society voted to establish a permanent division of social work to present a program at the annual meetings.

ing about contact between the two groups. The struggle is not over when that step has been taken, for the school of social work has to prove its claims to academic status and respect, every inch of the way. The evolutionary process might be considerably expedited if the social scientists had an attitude of active coöperation towards developing an educational program for social work and felt that they were on the inside rather than on the outside of the venture. If they once accepted the idea that social work activities—somewhat changed and conducted in a scientific spirit, of course—might be an asset to social science, the motive for assuming a positive role would be supplied.

If the schools of social work live up to the opportunity afforded them by a friendly attitude on the part of the social scientists, they should open up channels with the local social organizations of value both to the schools of social work and to the social science departments. Nor should the school always act as intermediary. Direct relationships with social organizations would soon be independently developed by social scientists. Already such relationships have been set up in several universities. For some time members of university faculties have been serving as advisers and leaders upon community problems; the reverse process of using the community to enrich university courses and research has not been so marked a development but is gaining ground.

Social workers on the job must be educated to work with social scientists. The most obvious way to accomplish this in the future is to provide training for social workers within a university where the social science departments participate in directing the course. Furthermore, university students in general should be imbued with the idea of the relationship between social work and the social sciences, for many of them will have some contact with the field of social work. It is patent, however, that for some time to come the greater number of those directing social organizations will have had no specific education for their work. Those on the job must be reached through conferences, publications, and personal contacts. Certainly, some of them will recognize the reasons for the scientist's asking assistance in collecting social data; from this number a few capable of assisting will undoubtedly emerge.[19] The actual working out of coöperative undertakings will differ to considerable degree with the individual project, but in general the social worker must adapt his procedure of collecting and recording facts to form suited for use by the scientists. In return for this service, he should receive some interpretation of these data, or even suggestions of treatment, from the scientist. The research program of the scientist and the welfare program of the social worker will remain two distinct entities but with an area of overlapping interest. In time, this area of common endeavor may be almost indefinitely extended.

An important corollary to close relationships between the social sciences and social welfare programs would be that the social sciences would be drawn as a group into contact with practical affairs. Such contact would inevitably result in recognition of the problems com-

[19] See Frankel, "Measuring Sticks for Social Work," *Hospital Social Service*, XIV (October, 1926), 277-284.

mon to all social science, and should lead to coöperative research among its several divisions. Since in actual life it is often impossible to separate the psychological aspect of a problem from its economic aspect, or the legal aspect from either of the others, social scientists must of necessity synchronize their work when they turn from academic problems to those presented by the world about them.[20] Such work assumes that there is interest in understanding the entire problem, rather than in breaking it into meaningless parts—meaningless, that is, as a method of solving the problem. Joint effort on the part of political scientists, historians, psychologists, economists, and sociologists will be necessary before a social science capable of interpreting social life and directing social progress is created. As Dr. Merriam said in his presidential address before the American Political Science Association, December 1925, "The problem of social behavior is essentially one problem, and, while the angles of approach may and should be different, the scientific result will be imperfect unless these points of view are at times brought together in some effective way so that the full benefit of the multiple analysis may be realized."[21]

Until this multiple analysis is undertaken, social

[20] "Likewise we are likely to see a closer integration of the social sciences themselves, which in the necessary process of differentiation have in many cases become too much isolated. In dealing with basic problems, such as those of the punishment and prevention of crime, alcoholism, the vexed question of human migration, the relations of the negro, and a wide variety of industrial and agricultural problems, it becomes evident that neither the facts and the technique of economics alone, nor of politics alone, nor of history alone, are adequate to their analysis and interpretation." Merriam, "Progress in Political Research," *The American Political Science Review*, XX (Feb. 1926), 8.

[21] *Ibid.*, p. 9.

welfare programs can derive little benefit from the uncorrelated findings of the various social sciences. Once granted that social scientists accept joint responsibility for leadership in framing a program of social welfare, joint study and research will inevitably follow. Recognition of joint interests would probably result in modified research programs for the individual social sciences. Not only would group problems tend to take priority over those with prime interest only for one science, but also the approach and method of handling a problem by a particular science might be quite different if effort were made to dovetail with other sciences.

The social scientists will not complete their task by working out satisfactory relationships among themselves and with social workers. Relationships with the natural sciences must also be clarified, for there are social and political implications of natural science which condition the central problem of human behavior.[22] It was said above that the psychological, legal, and economic aspects of a problem may be inextricably interwoven; the physiological aspect is as often vitally influenced by these other factors and, in turn, may influence each of them. Nor is it possible to plan for human welfare without taking into account what effect developments in physics, chemistry, medicine, agriculture, industry, etc., may have upon social life.

[22] "Still more serious for the student of politics is the integration of social science with the results of what is called natural science—the reunion of the natural and the 'non-natural' sciences. For more and more it appears that the last word in human behavior is to be scientific; more and more clearly it becomes evident that the social and political implications of natural science are of fundamental importance." *Ibid.,* p. 9.

Close contact between social and natural scientists with something resembling an integrated program of social research must be realized.[23] The impetus for developing such research is regarded as inevitable when existing social problems are approached with the idea of finding remedies. As long as each science or each division of science concentrates on shaping its own program of research in terms of the knowledge and problems of its own field, there will be little light shed on the central problem of human behavior. One can as well imagine a symphony being composed with each player given the task of writing his own part to develop his instrument's full capacity.

A program of social welfare which will elicit the interest and coöperation of scientists is therefore needed. Not a detailed program, naturally, since the chief value of association between social workers[24] and scientists will lie in opportunity given for modifying procedure on the basis of research findings, but a program that indicates the ways in which science can contribute and can derive benefit from an alliance with active organizations. Leadership must be taken by scientists, or by social workers, or by the public in shaping a program which will draw together all the

[23] "The particular pattern of problem, the special form of technique, whether statistical or anthropological or psychological or other-logical, is not important; or what the product is labelled. But this is fundamental— that politics and social sciences see face to face; that social science and natural science come together in a common effort and unite their forces in the greatest task that humanity has yet faced—the intelligent understanding and control of human behavior." *Ibid.*, p. 12.

[24] Broadly interpreted to mean those persons actively promoting social welfare through various types of organizations interested in public welfare, health, recreation, family integrity, etc.

factors necessary for its realization. In brief, some one must turn executive, accepting responsibility for pointing out the functions which each group must assume, and able to demonstrate the soundness, or at least the logic, of his plans to the public, to the social workers, to the scientists. Such a leader must have knowledge of the scope of each professional group whose services he commands, and must have the particular ability to mold their various contributions into a coherent, functioning whole. Assignment of suitable responsibilities to social work would become a simple task for one so equipped. He would have as his general objective the promotion of social welfare, in the achievement of which he must take account of each element of social welfare, and how these elements might best be combined to serve the general objective. The rôle to be filled seems in large part unlike that of social worker, or scientist, or lay citizen. Breadth of interest and knowledge, executive ability, power of leadership, imagination, and creative planning are requisite. A new profession, or perhaps a new type of individual, may be required to take over responsibilities not now met by any existing group. A new name has appeared in advance of claimants for the title— "social engineering." The public interest lies in developing or discovering social engineers who will give meaning to this new term.

In conclusion it may be said that the destiny of social work should be determined primarily by developments in the social sciences. Guidance for social work must come from this direction, since a constructive program can be based only upon knowlege and understanding of the meaning of social phenomena. Social work deals directly with the results of social phenomena and can contribute out of this experience to the analysis of social problems. Assistance is needed, however, in indicating what problems have important social as well as individual implications, what methods of treatment will yield data for the study and ultimate solution of these problems. Supplying such data will be one of the primary obligations of social work when channels have been created to bring its first-hand experiences with social life to the attention of the scientists. In addition, there will still be responsibility for relief of the distressed and for solving immediate problems of adjustment, while the major questions of the future solution of social problems are left to the scientist and to the statesman.

PERIODICALS AND PUBLICATIONS

IN THE FIELD OF SOCIAL WELFARE AND APPLIED SOCIAL SCIENCE

Key to abbreviations:　(Q)　Quarterly
　　　　　　　　　　　(M)　Monthly
　　　　　　　　　　　(W)　Weekly
　　　　　　　　　　　(Bi-M)　Bi-Monthly

American Economic Review　(Q)
　American Economic Association. Evanston, Ill.
American Journal of Psychiatry　(Bi-M)
　American Psychiatric Association. Baltimore, Md.
American Journal of Psychology　(Q)
　Cornell University. Ithaca, N. Y.
American Journal of Public Health　(M)
　American Public Health Association. New York City.
American Journal of Sociology　(Bi-M)
　American Sociological Society. Chicago, Ill.
Annals of the American Academy of Political and Social Science　(Q)
　American Academy of Political and Social Science. Philadelphia, Pa.
Better Times　(W)
　Better Times, Inc. New York City.
Bulletin of American Association for Organizing Family Social Work　(Q)
　American Association for Organizing Family Social Work. New York City.
Child Health Bulletin　(M)
　American Child Health Association. New York City.
Child Welfare Magazine　(M)
　Child Welfare Co. Germantown, Pa.
Child Welfare News Summary　(W)
　U. S. Children's Bureau. Washington, D. C.

Children   (M)
> Parents' Publishing Co. New York City.

Community Center   (Bi-M)
> National Community Center Association. New York City.

Compass, The   (M)
> American Association of Social Workers. New York City.

Family, The   (M)
> American Association for Organizing Family Social Work. New York City.

Hospital Social Service   (M)
> Hospital Social Service Association. New York City.

Hygeia   (M)
> American Medical Association. Chicago, Ill.

Industrial Psychology   (M)
> Colgate University. Hamilton, N. Y.

International Labour Review   (M)
> International Labour Office. Geneva, Switzerland.

Jewish Social Science Quarterly   (Q)
> National Conference of Jewish Social Work. New York City.

Journal of Abnormal and Social Psychology   (Q)
> American Psychological Association. New York City.

Journal of American Statistical Association   (Q)
> American Statistical Association. New York City.

Journal of Delinquency   (Bi-M)
> Whittier State School. Whittier, Cal.

Journal of Home Economics   (M)
> American Home Economics Association. Baltimore, Md.

Journal of Political Economy   (Bi-M)
> University of Chicago. Chicago, Ill.

Journal of Social Hygiene   (M)
> American Social Hygiene Association. New York City.

Junior Red Cross News   (M)
> American Junior Red Cross. Washington, D. C.

Mental Hygiene (Q)
> National Committee for Mental Hygiene. New York City.

Mental Hygiene Bulletin (M)
> National Committee for Mental Hygiene. New York City.

Modern Hospital (M)
> Modern Hospital Publishing Co. Chicago, Ill.

Monthly Labor Review (M)
> U. S. Bureau of Labor Statistics. Washington, D. C.

National Catholic Welfare Conference Bulletin (M)
> National Catholic Welfare Conference. Washington, D. C.

National Conference of Social Work Bulletin (Q)
> National Conference of Social Work. Cincinnati, O.

National Conference of Social Work Proceedings (Annual)
> National Conference of Social Work. Cincinnati, O.

National Municipal Review (M)
> National Municipal League. New York City.

Nation's Health (M)
> Modern Hospital Publishing Co. Chicago, Ill.

News Bulletin
> Association of Community Chests and Councils. New York City.

News Bulletin
> National Bureau of Economic Research. New York City.

Opportunity (M)
> National Urban League. New York City.

Playground (M)
> Playground and Recreation Association of America. New York City.

Political Science Quarterly (Q)
> Academy of Political Science. Columbia University. New York City.

Psychiatric Quarterly, The (Q)
> State Department of Mental Hygiene. Albany, N. Y.

Quarterly Journal of Economics (Q)
> Harvard University. Cambridge, Mass.

Red Cross Courier (W)
> American Red Cross. Washington, D. C.

Revue Internationale de l'Enfant (M)
> Union Internationale de Secours aux Enfants. Geneva, Switzerland.

Social Forces (Q)
> University of North Carolina Press. Chapel Hill, N. C.

Social Science (Q)
> Pi Gamma Mu National Social Science Honor Society. Winfield, Kan.

Social Service Review (Q)
> University of Chicago. Chicago, Ill.

Social Welfare
> Social Service Council of Canada. Toronto, Can.

Sociological Review (Q)
> Sociological Society. London, England.

Sociology and Social Research (Bi-M)
> University of Southern California. Los Angeles, Cal.

Southwestern Political and Social Science Quarterly (Q)
> Southwestern Political and Social Science Association. Austin, Tex.

Statistical Bulletin (M)
> Metropolitan Life Insurance Co. New York City.

Survey and *Survey Graphic* (Semi-M)
> Survey Associates, Inc. New York City.

Social Worker
> Simmons College School of Social Work Alumnæ. Boston, Mass.

Welfare (M)
> State Department of Public Welfare. Springfield, Ill.

BIBLIOGRAPHY

The abbreviations used in the Bibliography refer to the publications of the following organizations:

N. C. S. W.—National Conference of Social Workers.
N. C. C. C.—National Conference of Catholic Charities.
N. C. J. C.—National Conference of Jewish Charities.
A. A. S. W.—American Association of Social Workers.

SELECTED AND REPRESENTATIVE
BIBLIOGRAPHY

UNDERLYING PHILOSOPHY
Books

Addams, Jane, Woods, R. A., and others, *Philanthropy and Social Progress*. Thomas Y. Crowell Co., 1893.

Cabot, R. C. (Ed.), *The Goal of Social Work*. Houghton Mifflin Co., 1927. *Social Service and the Art of Healing*. Moffat, Yard & Co., 1915. *What Men Live By*. Rev. ed. Houghton Mifflin Co., 1926.

Carver, T. N., *Essays in Social Justice*. Harvard Univ. Press, 1915. *Sociology and Social Progress*. Ginn & Co., 1912.

Carver, T. N., and Hall, H. B., *Human Relations*. D. C. Heath & Co., 1923.

Cheyney, Alice S., *A Definition of Social Work*. Univ. of Pennsylvania Press, 1923.

Cooley, C. H., *Human Nature and the Social Order*. Charles Scribner's Sons, 1902.

De Schweinitz, Karl, *Art of Helping People Out of Trouble*. Houghton Mifflin Co., 1924.

Devine, E. T., "Constructive Philanthropy," in Ward, H. F., *Social Ministry*. Eaton & Mains, 1910. *Misery and Its Causes*. Macmillan, 1913.

Dewey, John, *Human Nature and Conduct.* Henry Holt & Co., 1922.

Fairchild, H. P., *The Foundations of Social Life.* Wiley, 1927.

Groves, E. R., *Personality and Social Adjustment.* Longmans, Green & Co., 1923.

Hart, Hornell, *Science of Social Relations.* Henry Holt & Co., 1927.

Kellar, A. G., *Starting-Points in Social Science.* Ginn & Co., 1925.

Lindeman, E. C., *Social Discovery.* Republic Publishing Co., 1924.

MacFarland, C. S., *Spiritual Culture and Social Service.* Fleming H. Revell Co., 1912.

MacKenzie, J. S., *Outlines of Social Philosophy.* Macmillan, 1919.

Mecklin, J. M., *Introduction to Social Ethics.* Harcourt, Brace & Co., 1920.

Menge, E. J., *Backgrounds for Social Workers.* R. G. Badger, 1918.

Noble, Edmund, *Purposive Evolution.* Henry Holt & Co., 1926.

Odum, H. W., *Man's Quest for Social Guidance.* Henry Holt & Co., 1927.

Ogburn, W. F., and Goldenweiser, A., *The Social Sciences and Their Interrelations.* Houghton Mifflin Co., 1927.

Queen, Stuart, *Social Work in the Light of History.* J. B. Lippincott Co., 1922.

Sidis, B., *Source and Aim of Human Progress.* R. G. Badger, 1919.

Southard, E. E., and Jarrett, M. C., *The Kingdom of Evils.* Macmillan, 1922.

Street, Elwood, *Sympathy and System in Giving.* A. C. McClurg & Co., 1921.

Sumner, W. G., *What Social Classes Owe to Each Other.* New ed., Harper & Brothers, 1920.

Todd, A. J., *Theories of Social Progress*. Macmillan, 1918. *Scientific Spirit and Social Work*. Macmillan, 1919.

Wallas, Graham, *Our Social Heritage*. Yale Univ. Press, 1921.

White, W. C., and Heath, L. J., *New Basis for Social Progress*. Houghton Mifflin Co., 1917.

Williams, J. M., *Foundations of Social Science*. Alfred A. Knopf, 1920.

Williams, Whiting. *Mainsprings of Men*. Charles Scribner's Sons, 1925.

Periodical Articles and Pamphlets

Baldwin, Roger N., "Social Work and the Labor Movement," *Hospital Social Service*, XIV, No. 4, pp. 269-76.

Bruno, F. J., "Understanding Human Nature," *The Family*, VIII, No. 2, pp. 58 seq.

Cabot, R. C., "Ethics and Social Work," *The Survey*, LVI, 572-76.

Carter, L. E., "Governmental Responsibility in the Field of Social and Welfare Work," *N. C. S. W.*, 1926, pp. 457-60.

Eliot, T. D., "Permanency of Responsibility in Social Work," *Social Forces*, II, 506-12.

"Ethics of the Professions and of Business," *Annals of the American Academy*, CI, 167-68.

Flexner, Abraham, "Is Social Work a Profession?" *N. C. S. W.*, 1915, pp. 576-90.

Folks, Homer, "Public and Private—and Both," *The Survey*, LV, 137-38.

Hart, Hastings H., "Spiritual Dynamics of Social Work," Commencement address at Wilberforce Univ., June 17, 1915.

Hart, Hornell, "Jesus as a Social Worker," *Welfare*, XVIII, 1279-86.

Hocking, W. E., "Osmosis: the Object of Social Work," *The Survey*, LV, 361-62 .

Hodson, Wm., "Is Social Work Professional? A Re-examination of the Question," *N. C. S. W.*, 1925.

Karpf, M. J., "The Development of the Relation Between Sociology and Social Work," *Am. Sociological Society*, Univ. of Chicago Press, 1927, XXI, 213-22. "Relation Between Sociology and Social Work," *Social Forces*, III, 419-27.

Keppel, F. P., "The Future of the Social Movement," *The Family*, VIII, 97-99.

Lapp, J. A., "Justice First," *N. C. S. W.*, 1927.

Lindeman, E. C., "The Social Worker and His Community," *The Survey*, LII, 83-85. "The Social Worker as a Prophet," *The Survey*, LII, 346. "The Social Worker as a Statesman," *The Survey*, LII, 222-24.

Riddick, Helen, "The Relation of Sociology to Social Work," *The Family*, VIII, 353-59.

Ryan, John, "The Spiritual Element in Social Work," *Hospital Social Service*, XIV, 351-61.

Smith, Geddes, "Behemoth Walks Again," *The Survey*, LVI, 359-61.

Woods, A. E., "Cultural Values in the Social Service Curriculum." Unpublished paper. "Whither Social Work?" *The Survey*, LVIII, 74-75.

DESCRIPTION AND DISCUSSION OF PRESENT METHODS

Books

Allen, W. H., *Efficient Democracy*. Dodd, Mead & Co., 1907.

Bogen, B. D., *Jewish Philanthropy*. Macmillan, 1917.

Devine, E. T., *The Family and Social Work*. Survey Associates, 1912. *Social Work*. Macmillan, 1922.

Devine, E. T., and Brandt, L., *American Social Work in the Twentieth Century*. Frontier Press, 1921.

Kelso, R. W., *Science of Public Welfare*. Henry Holt & Co., 1927.

Lapp, J. A., *Practical Social Science*. Macmillan, 1926.

Lumley, F. E., *Means of Social Control*. The Century Co., 1925.

Norton, W. J., *Coöperative Movement in Social Work*. Macmillan, 1927.

Odum, H. W., *An Approach to Public Welfare and Social Work*. Univ. of North Carolina Press, 1926.

Towne, E. T., *Social Problems*. Rev. ed. Macmillan, 1924.

Townsend, Harriet, *Social Work, a Family Builder*. W. B. Saunders Co., 1926.

Warner, A. G., *American Charities*. Thomas Y. Crowell Co., 1894.

Watson, F. D., *The Charity Organization Movement in the United States*. Macmillan, 1922.

Webb, Sidney and Beatrice, *The Prevention of Destitution*. Longmans, Green & Co., 1911.

Woods, R. A., and Kennedy, A. J., *Settlement Horizon*. Russell Sage Foundation, 1922.

Periodical Articles and Pamphlets

Adie, D. C., "Relations of Public and Private Case Work Agencies," *The Family*, V, 247-51.

Almy, Frederic, "The Relationships of Public and Private Charities," *N. C. S. W.*, 1916.

Bowen, G. M., "Interpretative Publicity as a Function of Social Work: What Part Can the (Welfare) Federation Take in Its Development?" *N. C. S. W.*, 1924.

Bowman, H. C., "The Proper Division of Charitable Work Between Public and Private Agencies," *N. C. S. W.*, 1909.

Bowman, L. E., "What the Press Thinks of Social Work," *N. C. S. W.*, 1923.

Bradway, J. S., "The Use by Social Workers of Legal Resources in Constructing Social Programs," *Hospital Social Service*, XVI, 385.

Breckinridge, S. P., "The Public Profession of Social Work." Address delivered at Vassar College, April, 1926.

Brisley, M. S., "Community Chest Corollaries," *The Survey*, LIV, 344-46.

Brown, J. R., "Publicity versus Propaganda in Family Work," *The Family*, VII, 75-79.

Bruno, F. J., "Unit Cost of Service in a Case Working Agency," *The Family*, IV, 89-91. "Objective Tests in Case Work." *N. C. S. W.*, 1926.

Callahan, P. H., "Should Religious Organizations be Included in Community Chests?" *Catholic Charities Review*, IX, 375-77.

"Can C. O. S. Salaries be Standardized?" *The Survey*, XLI, 703.

Chapman, F. E., "The Community Chest—Its Advantages and Disadvantages," *Modern Hospital*, XX, 523-25.

Cheyney, Alice S., *The Nature and Scope of Social Work*. A. A. S. W., N. Y., 1926. Pamphlet.

Clapp, Raymond, "Job and Salary Analysis in Social Work," *N. C. S. W.*, 1921.

Dale, J. A., "What the Conference Gave Canada," *The Survey*, LII, 439-40.

Davis, O. W., "Process of Standardization Among Social Agencies," *N. C. S. W.*, 1920.

Dunham, Arthur, "The Executive and His Job," *Better Times*, Feb. 2, 1925. "Job Specifications in Social Work," *ibid.*, June 1, 1925. "The Organization of Social Agencies," *ibid.*, Oct. 6, 1924.

Folks, Homer, "What Canada Gave the Conference," *The Survey*, III, 440-41.

Frankel, Emil, "Measuring Sticks for Social Work," *Hospital Social Service*, XIV, 277-84.

Friedman, Rev. W. S., "State Supervision of Private Charities," *N. C. S. W.*, 1911.

Geier, F. A., "A Business Man's Criticism of the Present Organization of Social Service," *N. C. S. W.*, 1917.

Gillin, J. L., "Popular Presentation of Public Work," *N. C. S. W.*, 1925.

Hagerty, J. E., and others, "The Relation of Diocesan Charitable and Social Activities to Community Organizations," *N. C. C. C.*, 1920.

Haynes, Rowland C., "Relation of Scientific Research and the Development and Administration of Social Work," *The Family*, VII, 173.

Hill, Norah, "Social Work and Politics," *Hospital Social Service*, XIV, 223-26.

Hunter, Estelle B., *Office Administration*. Pamphlet. U. S. Children's Bureau Publication 101, Washington. Government Printing Office, 1922.

Ihlder, John, *Social Agencies and the Community*, Pamphlet. Civic Development Dept., Chamber of Commerce of the U. S., Washington, 1922.

Jackson, James F., *Relationship between a Board of Directors and the Professional Social Worker*. Pamphlet. School of Applied Social Sciences, Western Reserve University.

Johnson, Alexander, "On Being a Director (Charity Organization Dept., Russell Sage Foundation): An Open Letter to Directors," *The Survey*, XXIV, 135-36.

Johnson, Charles H., "Correlation of Public and Private Social Service," *N. C. S. W.*, 1924, pp. 29-34.

Johnson, Charles H., and others, "Coöperation and Relation of Public and Private Agencies," *Tenth N. Y. C. Conf. of Charities and Correction*, 1919, pp. 69-76.

Johnston, G. A., "Social Work and Labour Legislation," *International Labour Review*, XVI, 449-71.

Jones, Cheney C., "Relation of Private Societies to Juvenile Courts and to State Bureaus of Protection," *N. C. S. W.*, 1915, pp. 149-63.

Karpf, Maurice J., *A Social Audit of a Social Agency: the Jewish Aid Society and the Jewish Social Service Bureau of Chicago, 1919 to 1925*. Pamphlet. Chicago, 1925.

Keegan, Rev. Robert F., "Relations between the Church and the Public Authorities in the Supervision of Private Organizations in New York," *N. C. S. W.*, 1926, pp. 515-19.

Kelso, Robert W., "Benevolence—Boston Style," *The Survey*, LII, 343-46. "Is There a Dividing Line Between the Cases Which the Public Agency Should Take Over, and Those Which Should Be Handled by Private Social Agencies?" *N. C. S. W.*, 1921, pp. 215-18. "Public Welfare—Whose Responsibility? How City and Private Agencies Share It in Boston," *National Municipal Review*, XIV, 233-39. "Policy of Issuing State Charters to Charities," *N. C. S. W.*, 1915, pp. 485-92. "What is a Social Work Executive?" *The Survey*, LVIII, 114-15.

Kelso, Robert W., and others, "Supervision and Licensing of Private Charities," *N. C. S. W.*, 1917, pp. 364-69.

Kingsbury, J. A., "Coördination of Official and Private Activity in Public Health Work," *N. C. S. W.*, 1913, pp. 169-73.

Klein, Philip, "Job Analysis in Social Work," *N.C.S.W.*, 1925, pp. 685-87. "Professional Service and Salaries in Public Welfare Departments," *Annals of The American Academy*, CXIII, 226-34.

Larmour, V. A., "Coöperation Between Public and Private Agencies," *Catholic Charities Review*, X, 345-47.

Logan, J. C., "The Coöperation of Public and Private Welfare Agencies," *Annals of the American Academy*, CV. 88-92. "Relation of Layman and Expert in Social Work," *Social Forces*, II, 492-97. "Uses and

Procedure of Committee Meetings in Social Work," *Social Forces*, I, 370-75.

McLean, F. H., *The Central Council of Social Agencies: A Manual.* Pamphlet. American Association for Organizing Family Social Work, N. Y., 1921. "The Central Council of Social Agencies: Actual Accomplishments," *N. C. S. W.*, 1921, pp. 432-38.

Miles, R. E., "Organization of Social Forces of the State," *N. C. S. W.*, 1920, pp. 27-33.

Norton, W. J., "Community Organization," *N. C. S. W.*, 1919, pp. 665-70. "Growing Demand for Coördination of National Social Work," *N. C. S. W.*, 1920, pp. 27-33. "Social Work in a Competitive World," *The Survey*, LIV, 431.

Park, R. E., "Methods of Forming Public Opinion Applicable to Social Welfare Publicity," *N. C. S. W.*, 1918, pp. 615-22.

"Popular Idea of Social Work," *Better Times*, Feb. 2, 1925, p. 13.

Pratt, G. K., "Youth and the Dragons," *The Survey*, LIII, 475-77.

Raymond, Stockton, "Shall Social Work Sell Its Birthright for a Mess of Pottage?" *Social Worker* (Alumnæ of Simmons School of Social Work) I, 15-17.

Routzahn, E. G., *Elements of a Social Publicity Program.* Pamphlet. Russell Sage Foundation, 1920.

Rubinow, I. M., "Social Case Work—A Profession in the Making," *Social Forces*, IV, 286-93.

Scott, Elmer, "Organizing the Social Forces of a State," *N. C. S. W.*, 1919.

Scott, Nell, "Fallacies in the Use of Statistics," *The Family*, V, 200-03.

Sears, Amelia, "The Psychology of Coöperation." *N. C. S. W.*, 1915.

Shirer, H. H., "Public and Private Charities," *N.C.S.W.* 1916.

Smith, Geddes, "The Self-Conscious Community, a Study of National-Local Relationships in Social Work," *The Survey*, L, 427-30.

Social Work: An Outline of Its Professional Aspects. Pamphlet. A. A. S. W., N. Y., 1922.

Van Kleeck, Mary, and Taylor, G. R., "The Professional Organization of Social Work," *Annals of the American Academy*, CI, 158-68.

Watson, F. D., "American Social Agencies and Social Progress," *Social Forces*, I, 87-90.

Webb, Sidney, "The Extension Ladder Theory of the Relation between Voluntary Philanthropy and State or Municipal Action," *The Survey*, XXXI, 703-07. Correspondence regarding Mr. Webb's article by Henderson, C. R., Sheffield, A., and Cross, W. T., *ibid.*, XXXII, 227-28.

SPECIAL TECHNIQUES

Books

Breckinridge, S. P., *Family Welfare Work in a Metropolitan Community.* Univ. of Chicago Press, 1924. *Public Welfare Administration in the United States.* Univ. of Chicago Press, 1927.

Breckinridge, S. P., and Abbott, Edith, *The Delinquent Child and the Home.* Charities Publishing Co., 1912.

Byington, M. F., *What Social Workers Should Know About Their Own Communities.* Russell Sage Foundation, 1924.

Chapin, F. S., *Introduction to the Study of Social Evolution.* The Century Co., 1913. *Historical Introduction to Social Economy.* The Century Co., 1917. *Field Work and Social Research.* The Century Co., 1920.

Clopper, E. N., *Child Labor in City Streets.* Macmillan, 1912.

Groves, E. R., *Social Problems of the Family.* J. B. Lippincott Co., 1927.

Harris, F. S., and Butt, N. I., *Scientific Research and Human Welfare*. Macmillan, 1924.

Hart, J. K., *Community Organization*. Macmillan, 1920. *Adult Education*. Thomas Y. Crowell Co., 1927.

Healy, Wm., and Bronner, A. F., *Delinquents and Criminals; Their Making and Unmaking*. Macmillan, 1926.

Kelly, E. T. (ed.), *Welfare Work in Industry*. Sir Isaac Pitman & Sons, 1925.

Kelso, Robert, *The Science of Public Welfare*. Henry Holt & Co., 1928.

Lou, H. H., *Juvenile Courts in the United States*. Univ. of North Carolina Press, 1927.

MacIver, R. M., *Community: A Sociological Study*. New ed. Macmillan, 1924.

Odum, H. W., and Willard, D. W., *Systems of Public Welfare*. Univ. of North Carolina Press, 1925.

Richmond, Mary, *Social Diagnosis*. Russell Sage Foundation, 1917. *What is Social Case Work?* Russell Sage Foundation, 1922.

Sheffield, Ada, *Social Case History*. Russell Sage Foundation, 1920.

Steiner, J. F., *Community Organization*. The Century Co., 1925. *The American Community in Action*. Henry Holt & Co., 1928.

Van Waters, Miriam, *Youth in Conflict*. Republic Publishing Co., 1925.

Wulkop, E., *Social Worker in a Hospital Ward*. Houghton Mifflin Co., 1926.

Periodical Articles and Pamphlets

Abbot, E. S., "What is Mental Hygiene?" *American Journal of Psychiatry*, IV, 263-64.

Adler, Jessie, "In the Courts," *The Survey*, LVI, 268.

Armstrong, R. G., "Wanted—a Technique for the Rural County," *The Survey*, LIX, 382-83.

Blackburn, Burr, "Health Education and Welfare Agencies in Georgia Counties," *Social Forces*, VI, 61.

Borst, H. W., "The County as a Unit in Charitable Administration," *N. C. S. W.*, 1918.

Brogden, M. S., *Handbook of Organization and Method in Hospital Social Service*. Johns Hopkins Hospital. Baltimore, 1922.

Bruno, F. J., "A Romance of Family Case Work," *The Survey*, LV, 87-89.

Burgess, E. W., "The Contribution of Sociology to Family Social Work," *The Family*, VIII, 191-93.

Burgess, E. W., "The Natural Area as the Unit for Social Work in the Large City," *N. C. S. W.*, 1926, pp. 504-10.

Byington, M. F., "Coördination of Civic Effort in Smaller Communities," *N. C. S. W.*, 1916, pp. 472-79. *The Confidential Exchange*. Pamphlet. Russell Sage Foundation, N. Y., 1912.

Cabot, H., "The Relation of Medical Social Service to the General Hospital Organization," *Hospital Social Service*, XI, 1-6.

Cannon, I. M., *Social Work in Hospitals*. Pamphlet. Russell Sage Foundation, N. Y., 1923.

Chesley, A. L., "Personal Aims and Methods in Social Case Work," *The Survey*, LV, 89-90.

Classification of Social Agencies by Function in the City of New York. N. Y. Welfare Council, 1926.

Content of Family Social Work. Pamphlet Report of a Committee of the American Assn. for Organizing Family Social Work, Quarterly Bulletin, June, 1926.

Curry, H. I., "The Status of Social Work in Rural Communities," *N. C. S. W.*, 1918, pp. 83-91. "The County as a Unit in Charity Experience," *N. C. S. W.*, 1918, pp. 241-44.

Davenport, W. H., "The County as a Unit in Charitable Administration," *ibid.*, pp. 240-50.

Davis, M. M., Jr., "Pay Clinics for Persons of Moderate Means," *N. C. S. W.*, 1915, pp. 228-36.

Devine, E. T., "Central Councils of Social Agencies," *The Survey*, XLVII, 624-26; *ibid.*, pp. 724-26.

Dinwiddie, C., *Community Responsibility: A Review of the Cincinnati Social Unit Experiment.* Pamphlet. N. Y. School of Social Work, 1921.

Donohoe, M. L., "Next Steps in State Hospital Social Service," *Mental Hygiene Bulletin*, Vol. II, Dec. 1924.

Edwards, A. L., "How Can the Home Economist Coöperate with the Local Family Case Worker?" *The Survey*, LVI, 391.

Glueck, B., "Special Preparation of the Psychiatric Social Worker," *N. C. S. W.*, 1919, pp. 599-606.

Hardwick, K. D., and Thurston, H. W., "Minimum Standards of Training for Family Case Work," *N. C. S. W.*, 1922, pp. 245-57.

Hewins, K. P., "Shaping the Record to Facilitate Research," *N. C. S. W.*, 1916, pp. 460-68.

Jacobs, T., "Progress in Work with the Family," *Social Forces*, VI, 55.

Jarrett, M. C., "The Need for Research in Social Case Work by Experienced Social Workers Who Are Themselves Doing the Case Work," *Social Forces*, III, 668-69.

Jensen, H. E., "The County as an Administrative Unit in Social Work," *Social Forces*, II, 552-59.

Lee, P., (ed.), *Vocational Aspects of Psychiatric Social Work.* Pamphlet. *A. A. S. W.*, N. Y., 1926. *Vocational Aspects of Family Social Work. A. A. S. W.*, N. Y., 1926. *Vocational Aspects of Medical Social Work. A. A. S. W.*, N. Y., 1927. Pamphlet.

MacKay, E. H., "Organization and Supervision of Field Work from the Viewpoint of the Social Agency," *The Family*, V, 253-56.

McClenahan, B. A., "County Organization of Welfare Agencies," *N. C. S. W.*, 1918, pp. 595-604.

McLean, F., *Enlarged Future Program of Our Movement and Name of Our Association*. Pamphlet. American Assn. of Societies for Organizing Family Social Work, N. Y., 1918. *The Organization of Family Social Work Societies in Smaller Cities*. Pamphlet. American Assn. for Organizing Family Social Work, N. Y., 1923.

Marriner, J. L., "Coördination of Public and Private Agencies in a State Program of Public Health Nursing," *N. C. S. W.*, 1920, pp. 204-08.

Matthews, H. J., "Special Problems of Rural Social Work," *Social Forces*, VI, 67.

Meredith, F., "Medical Training for Social Workers," *Nation's Health*, IV, 20-22.

Morgan, E. D., "Organizing a County," *N. C. S. W.*, 1919, pp. 695-97.

"Mothers' Allowances in North America," *International Labour Review*, Nov., 1927.

"Principles of Hospital Administration and the Training of Hospital Executives," *Hospital Social Service*, April, 1922.

Queen, S. A., "Some Possible Sociological Uses of the Case Work Method," *Journal of Applied Sociology*, XI, 322-26.

Reynolds, B. C., "A Quest for Treatment Processes in Social Work," *Hospital Social Service*, Vol. XIV, Dec., 1926.

Reynolds, W. S., "Case Conference: Need and Plan," *N. C. S. W.*, 1919, pp. 336-38.

Sheffield, A. E., *Case Work in Public Welfare Departments; The Social Case History, its Construction and Content*. Pamphlet. Boston, 1920. *The Charity Director*. Pamphlet, Russell Sage Foundation, Charity Organization Dept., 1916.

Sign-Posts: Report of the Field Dept. of the American Association for Organizing Family Social Work, Sept. 1927. Pamphlet.

Steiner, J. F., "Basis of Procedure in Rural Social Work," *Social Forces*, IV, 504-09.

Taft, J., "Qualifications of the Psychiatric Social Worker," *N. C. S. W.*, 1919, pp. 593-99.

Terpinning, W. A., *Social Organizations Working with Rural People*. Extension Dept., Western State Normal School. Kalamazoo, Wis., 1926.

Todd, A. J., "Essential Sociological Equipment of Workers with Delinquents," *Social Hygiene*, VII, 13-21.

Tousley, C. M., "Interpretation of Case Work by the Case Work Method," *The Family*, VIII, 175-82.

Training for Hospital Social Work. Pamphlet. Report of Committee of American Hospital Assn. Bulletin No. 55. N. Y., 1923.

Ward, M. E., "Visiting Housekeeper Work in Detroit," *Mother and Child*, Nov., 1923, pp. 523-27.

TRAINING AND PERSONNEL

Books

Attlee, C. R., *The Social Worker*. Macmillan, 1920.

Bennett, H. C., *American Women in Social Work*. Dodd, Mead & Co., 1915.

Devine, E. T., *Social Work*. Macmillan, 1922.

Devine, E. T., and Van Kleeck, M., *Positions in Social Work*. N. Y. School of Social Work, 1916.

Hatcher, O. L., (ed.), *Occupations for Women*. Southern Woman's Educational Alliance. Atlanta, 1927.

Macadam, Elizabeth, *The Equipment of the Social Worker*. Henry Holt & Co., 1925.

Steiner, J. F., *Education for Social Work*. Univ. of Chicago Press, 1921.

Tead, Ordway, and Metcalf, H. C., *Personnel Administration*. McGraw Publishing Co., 1926.

Tufts, J. H., *Education and Training for Social Work*. Russell Sage Foundation, 1923.

Periodical Articles and Pamphlets

Abbott, Edith, "Field Work and the Training of the Social Worker," *N. C. S. W.*, 1915, pp. 615-21.

Addams, Jane, "Call of the Social Field," *N. C. S. W.*, 1911, pp. 370-72.

American Assn. of Social Workers Directory of Members. N. Y., 1925. Pamphlet.

Beisser, Paul, *A Measurement of Professional Training; Deductions from a Questionnaire Study of Social Work Positions*. Pamphlet. *A. A. S. W.*, N. Y., 1923.

Bogardus, Emory S., *Methods of Training Social Workers*. Pamphlet. Southern California Sociological Society. Los Angeles, 1921.

Bogen, Boris D, and others, "The Relation of a Social Worker to His Organization," *N. C. J. C.*, 1910, pp. 254-74.

Brackett, J. R., "The Curriculum of the Professional School of Social Work," *N. C. S. W.*, 1915, pp. 610-12.

Breckinridge, S. P., "Report of the Committee on Training Social Workers," *N. C. S. W.*, 1911, pp. 366-70.

Burnett, M. C., "Recruiting of Students by Schools and of Apprentices by Agencies," *N. C. S. W.*, 1926, pp. 599-607. "Salaries for New Recruits," *The Survey*, LVII, 395-96.

"California Defines Social Work," (bill introduced in legislature for examination and registration of social workers), *The Survey*, XLVI, 38-39.

Carroll, Mollie Ray, "Some Problems in the Training of Social Workers," *Social Forces*, I, 547-50.

Chapin, F. Stuart, "The University and Training for Social Work," *Social Forces*, I, 391-93.

Colcord, Joanna C., "On the Hiring Line," *The Family*, I, 6-15, 23-26. "Some Random Observations of Personnel Policy," *Compass*, VI, 2-5. "Who Pays for Training?" *Compass*, VI. 5.

"Conditions of Employment," *The Family*, I, 23.

Conrad, Sherman, "Labor Turnover in Social Agencies," *N. C. S. W.*, 1920, pp. 427-31.

Coulter, Charles W., "After College, What? Shall it be Professional or Private Social Work?" *Welfare*, XVIII, 289-94.

Cutler, J. E., *Training for Social Work; the correlation of the profession of social work and the university in the control of training schools*. School of Applied Science, Cleveland, 1922. Pamphlet.

Deardorff, Neva R., "A Restatement of the Objectives of Social Work Education," *Social Forces*, III, 237-41. "Education of Social Workers," *Annals of American Academy*, Sept., 1925.

De Morsier, J. M., "Les Ecoles Sociales," *Revue Internationale de l'Enfant*, I, 194-212.

Devine, Edward T., "Education for Social Work," *N. C. S. W.*, 1915, pp. 606-10.

Eliot, Thomas D., "Sociology as a Prevocational Subject: The Verdict of Sixty Social Workers," *Journal of Sociology*, XXIX, 744-54.

Emmet, Boris, *The Turnover of Labor*. U. S. Federal Board for Vocational Education, Bulletin 46. Washington, 1919. Pamphlet.

Eubank, Earle E., "Education for Social Work: Why and How." *Journal of Applied Sociology*, VIII, 164-70. "Toward Professional Social Work," *The Survey*, LV, 362-64.

"Expenditures and Salaries of Case Workers," *The Family*, I, 5-8, 11-16.

Folks, Homer, "Social Service Training," *American Journal of Public Health*, XIV, 479.

Foster, Edith, "Report of the First Training Course for Social Workers," *Wisconsin State Conference of Social Work*, 1922, pp. 120-23.

Frankfurter, Felix, "Social Work and Professional Training," *N. C. S. W.*, 1915, pp. 591-96.

Geer, Ellen W., "The Place of the Volunteer," *The Survey*, LVII, 392-93.

Gillin, J. L., "The Tufts Report on Education and Training for Social Work," *Social Forces*, I, 383-90. "The Objectives of Social Work Education," *Social Forces*, III, 408-13.

Goodwille, Mary C., "Efficiency in the Use of Volunteers," *N. C. S. W.*, 1915, pp. 83-88; *ibid.*, 1917, pp. 116-18.

Hagerty, James E., "Universities and Training for Public Leadership and Social Work," *Annals of the American Academy*, CV, 162-64. "The Undergraduate School of Social Work," *Catholic Charities Review*, IX, 91-94.

"How to Make Volunteer Workers More Useful," *Better Times*, Oct., 1921, pp. 29-30.

Hurlin, Ralph G., "Measuring the Demand for Social Workers," *N. C. S. W.*, 1926, pp. 587-95. "Social Work Salaries," *The Survey*, LV, 556-58. "Social Work Stability," *The Survey*, LVII, 396. "The Demand for Social Workers," *N. C. S. W.*, 1926.

Johnson, Fred R., "Salary Standards in Social Work," *N. C. S. W.*, 1920, pp. 424-27.

Kaplan, H., "Training for Jewish Social Service," *Jewish Social Service*, X, 173-76.

Karpf, M. J., "The Relation of Schools of Social Work to Social Agencies," *N. C. S. W.*, 1925, pp. 650-58.

Kempton, Helen P., "Why the Volunteer?" *The Family*, III, 193-95.

"Labor Turnover in Mid-Western Social Work," *Compass*, VI, 2-3.

Lee, Porter R., "Committee Report: The Professional Basis of Social Work," *N. C. S. W.*, 1915, pp. 596-606. "Providing Teaching Material for the Training of Social Workers," *N. C. S. W.*, 1920, pp. 465-73. "The Common Problem of the Family Case Work Agencies and the Schools," *The Family*, II, 129-33.

McCrea, Roswell C., "The Professional School for Social Workers," *N. C. S. W.*, 1911, pp. 380-84.

McLean, Francis H., "Double Standards," *The Family*, II, 230-31.

Mangold, George B., "The Curriculum of Schools of Social Service," *N. C. S. W.*, 1915, pp. 612-15.

Mudgett, Mildred D., "The Use of Advanced Students in Field Work," *Social Forces*, I, 395-99. "The Undergraduate in Social Research," *The Family*, III, 65-69.

Odum, H. W., "Positions for Trained Social Workers in the Field of Public Welfare," *Annals of the American Academy*, CV, 182-84.

Professional Education for Social Work. Statement by the Executive Committee of the Assn. of Training Schools for Professional Social Work, N. Y., 1924. Pamphlet.

"Professional Education for Social Work," *School and Society*, LXXXXI, 234-35.

"Professional Training for Social Case Work" (summary of the findings of the 1921 Institute of Family Social Work), *The Family*, II, 134-35.

Proposed Study of Education for Social Work. Report of Joint Committee of the Assn. of Training Schools for Social Work and the American Association of Social Workers. *A. A. S. W.*, N. Y., 1925. Pamphlet.

Purcell-Guild, June, "Social Workers and the Law," *The Survey*, LVI, 626-27.

Queen, S. A., "Curriculum of a Training School for Social Work," *American Journal of Sociology*, XXVIII, 283-97.

Quinn, Lillian A., "Vocational Work of the Association," *Compass*, VI, 2-7.

"Recruiting for Social Work," *The Survey*, XLVII, 422-23.

Report of Special Committee on Salary Standards of Detroit Community Fund. Research Bureau of Associated Charities, N. Y., 1923. Pamphlet.

Robinson, Virginia P., "The Organization of Field Work in a Professional School," *The Family*, I, 1-7. "Education for a Profession-in-the-Making," *The Survey*, LII, 589-92.

"Salaries among Social Workers," *Compass*, VII, 2-3.

"Salary Schedule of the United Charities of Chicago," *Compass*, III, 220.

Salary Study and Classification of Positions. Cleveland Welfare Federation, 1924. Pamphlet.

Siedenburg, F., "Training for Social Work," *Catholic World*, CXIII, 320-27.

Slade, F. L., "The Young Volunteer and the Junior League Movement," *N. C. S. W.*, 1917, pp. 125-26.

"Social Work Market Outlined," *Compass*, April, 1924.

Spaulding, Edith R., "The Training School of Psychiatric Social Work at Smith College," *N. C. S. W.*, 1919, pp. 606-10.

Statement of American Assn. for Social Workers as to Need of Study of Training Schools for Social Workers. A. A. S. W., N. Y., 1923. Pamphlet.

Steiner, J. F., "Education for Social Work," *American Journal of Sociology*, XXVI, 475-518, 744-66. "Education for Social Work in Rural Communities," *Social Forces*, VI, 41.

Stillman, C. C., "Some Ethical Elements in Leadership in Social Work," *N. C. S. W.*, 1926, pp. 607-13.

Taussig, F., "Some Aspects of Social Case Work," *News Bulletin of the Bureau of Vocational Information*, III, No. 8.

Taylor, M., "The Volunteer in Social Work," *The Family*, VI, 205-8.

The Profession of Social Work. The National Social Workers' Exchange Committee on Vocational Information. *A. A. S. W.*, N. Y. Pamphlet (undated).

Todd, A. J., "Observations on Personnel Policy," *Compass*, Vol. VI, No. 2. "Principles of Personnel Work in Social Service Agencies," *The Family*, IV, 221-24.

Tousley, C. M., "The Volunteer Professional," *The Family*, I, 2-6.

Training for Social Work. Bureau of Vocational Information, N. Y. Reprint No. 22. Pamphlet.

"Training Schools and the Market," *Compass*, Nov., 1924.

Van Waters, Miriam, "Is the Agency or the Individual Primarily Responsible for the Professional Development of the Social Worker?" Unpublished paper, 1925.

Vogt, P. L., "Training for Rural Service," *American Journal of Sociology*, XXV, 562-67.

"Volunteer in Social Work," *The Ounce*, Jan. 1925.

Wilder, Veronica P., "Our Salaries," *Compass*, March, 1922, pp. 6-9.

Wyckoff, G. P., "Educating the Field Outside of Metropolitan Centers to Demand Trained Workers," *N. C. S. W.*, 1926, pp. 595-99.

COST AND FINANCING

Books

Allen, William H., *Modern Philanthropy, a Study of Efficient Appealing and Giving*. Dodd, Mead & Co., 1912.

Bogen, Boris D., *Jewish Philanthropy*. Macmillan, 1917.

Moulton, Harold J., *Financial Organization of Society*. Univ. of Chicago Press, 1925.

Proctor, Arthur W., and Schuck, Arthur A., *The Financing of Social Work*. A. W. Shaw Co., 1926.

Periodical Articles and Pamphlets

Bliss, Paul S., "Interpreting Professional Standards of Social Work to the Public from the Standpoint of the Community Fund," *N. C. S. W.*, 1926, pp. 669-78.

Bookman, C. M., "A Unified Program of Social Work as a Creator of Public Opinion," *N. C. S. W.*, 1919, pp. 516-20. "The Community Chest Movement—an Interpretation," *N. C. S. W.*, 1924, pp. 19-29.

Burns, Allen T., "Organization of Community Forces," *N. C. S. W.*, 1926. pp. 62-79.

Byall, J. Bruce, "Organizing a Community's Resources (The Philadelphia Children's Bureau)," *N. C. S. W.*, 1915, pp. 141-45.

Clapp, Raymond, "Relief in Nineteen Cities," *The Survey*, LVII, 209-11. *Study of Volume and Cost of Social Work, 1924: Tabulation of Income for Nineteen Cities.* Pamphlet. American Assn. for Community Organization. May 25, 1926. "Tax and Contribution Support of Social Work: Facts as Revealed by the Study of Volume and Cost of Social Work," *N. C. S. W.*, 1926, pp. 449-57.

Dawson, John B, "Rise of Relief-giving During the Past Five Years," *N. C. S. W.*, 1922, pp. 228-36.

De Forest, Charles M., "Where Shall We Get the Money?" *Social Forces*, II, 57-61.

Douglas, Paul and Dorothy, "What Can a Man Afford?" *American Economic Review*, XI, 1-95.

Dripps, Robert D., "The Policy of State Aid to Private Charities," *N. C. S. W.*, 1915, pp. 458-74.

Fetter, Frank A., "Subsidizing of Private Charities," *American Journal of Sociology*, VII, 359-85.

Halbert, L. A., "Municipal Aid to Private Charities," *N. C. S. W.*, 1916, pp. 391-92.

Haynes, Rowland, "Priority Scale for Social Work," *The Survey*, LI, 333-34.

Hodson, William, *Is Welfare Work Worth Its Cost?* Special bulletin of the Welfare Council of N. Y., Dec. 1927.

Holbrook, David H., "The Saturation Point in Giving," *The Woman's Press*, April, 1927.

Hurlin, Ralph G., "The Mounting Bill for Relief," *The Survey*, LVII, 207-09.

Johnson, Fred R., "The Ideals of Financial Federation," *N. C. S. W.*, 1917, pp. 507-10.

King, Edith S., and Frear, Augusta H., "Finances of New York's Social Work," *Better Times*, June 1, 1925, pp. 21-29.

Lewis, O. M., "Should 'Big Business' Control Social Work?" *Social Worker* (Alumnæ of Simmons School of Social Work), I, 18-19.

Mulry, Thomas M., "Public Aid to Private Institutions," *N. C. C. C.*, 1912, pp. 44-56.

Norton, William J., "The Bill for Benevolence," *The Survey*, LI, 183-85. "Voluntary Giving as a Factor in Social Finance," *The Survey*, LI, 374-77, 425. "What the Client Pays," *ibid.*, LI, 507-09.

Persons, W. Frank., *Central Financing of Social Agencies.* Columbus, 1922. Pamphlet. *Welfare Council of New York City.* N. Y., 1925. Pamphlet.

"Private Charitable Corporations and Public Funds" (editorial), *The Survey*, XXVII, 1391-92.

Purdy, Lawson, "How Much Social Work Can a Community Afford?—From a Social and Economic Point of View," *N. C. S. W.*, 1926, pp. 100-07. "Need and Value of the Budget System for Social Agencies," *The Family*, I, 10-13.

Williams, C. V., "Chartering and Fiscal Control by State Authority of Voluntary Charities," *N. C. S. W.*, 1916, pp. 321-26.

GENERAL
Books

Abbott, Edith, *Historical Aspects of the Immigration Problem.* Univ. of Chicago Press, 1926. *Immigration; Select Documents and Case Records.* Univ. of Chicago Press, 1924.

Adams, R., and Sumner, H. L., *Labor Problems*. Macmillan, 1914.

Allport, F. H., *Social Psychology*. Houghton Mifflin Co., 1924.

Barnes, Harry E., and others, *History and Prospects of the Social Sciences*. Alfred A. Knopf, 1925.

Bernard, L. L., *Introduction to Social Psychology*. Henry Holt & Co., 1926.

Bliss, W. D., and Binder, R. M., *New Encyclopædia of Social Reform*. Funk & Wagnalls Co., 1910.

Blum, Salomon, *Labor Economics*. Henry Holt & Co., 1925.

Bott, E. A., *Studies in Industrial Psychology*. Univ. of Toronto, 1920.

Breckinridge, S. P., *Public Welfare Administration in the United States*. Univ. of Chicago Press, 1927.

Brooks, J. G., *Labor's Challenge to the Social Order*. Macmillan, 1920.

Brunner, E. D., *Village Communities*. Geo. H. Doran, 1927.

Burgess, E. W., *Function of Socialization in Social Evolution*. Univ. of Chicago Press, 1916.

Carlton, F. T., *History and Problems of Organized Labor*. D. C. Heath, 1911.

Carver, T. N., *Present Economic Revolution in the United States*. Little, Brown & Co., 1925.

Chenery, W. L., *Industry and Human Welfare*. Macmillan, 1922.

Clark, J. B., *Social Justice Without Socialism*. Houghton Mifflin Co., 1914.

Cole, G. D. H., *Self-Government in Industry*. Frederick A. Stokes Co., 1920.

Commons, J. R., *Trade Unionsim and Labor Problems*. Ginn & Co., 1921.

Commons, J. R., and others, *History of Labor in the United States*. Macmillan, 1918.

Commons, J. R., and Andrews, J. B., *Principles of Labor Legislation*. Harper & Brothers, 1920.

Conklin, E. G., *Heredity and Environment*. Princeton Univ. Press, 1923.

Cooley, C. H., *Human Nature and the Social Order*. Rev. ed., Charles Scribner's Sons, 1922. *Life and the Student*. Alfred A. Knopf, 1927. *Social Progress*. Charles Scribner's Sons, 1918. *Social Organization*. Charles Scribner's Sons, 1909.

Croly, H. D., *Progressive Democracy*. Macmillan, 1914.

Crowther, Samuel, *Why Men Strike*. Doubleday, Page Co., 1920.

Davis, J., and Barnes, H. E., and others, *Introduction to Sociology and Readings*. D. C. Heath, 1927.

Dealey, J. Q., *Family in Its Sociological Aspects*. Houghton Mifflin Co., 1912.

Devine, E. T., *Efficiency and Relief*. Macmillan, 1906.

Douglas, P. H., *Wages and the Family*. Univ. of Chicago Press, 1925.

Douglas, Hitchcock, and Atkins, *The Worker in Modern Society*. Univ. of Chicago Press, 1923.

Downey, E. H., *Workmen's Compensation*. Macmillan, 1924.

Edie, L. D., *Economics: Principles and Problems*. Thomas Y. Crowell Co., 1926.

Elliot, Hugh, *Modern Science and Materialism*. Longmans, Green & Co., 1927.

Ellwood, C. A., *The Psychology of Human Society*. D. Appleton & Co., 1925.

Fairchild, H. P., *Immigration: A World Movement and Its American Significance*. Macmillan, 1913.

Faulkner, H. N., *American Economic History*. Harper & Brothers, 1924.

Feld, R. C., *Humanizing Industry*. E. P. Dutton & Co., 1920.

Fitch, J. A., *The Causes of Industrial Unrest*. Harper & Brothers, 1924.

Flexner, A., *Medical Education*. Macmillan, 1925.

Follett, M. P., *New State*. Longmans, Green & Co., 1918. *Creative Experience*. Longmans, Green & Co., 1924.

Ford, J. (ed.), *Social Problems and Social Policy*. Ginn & Co., 1923.

Frank, Glenn, *Politics of Industry*. The Century Co., 1919.

Furniss, E. S., and Guild, L. I., *Labor Problems*. Houghton Mifflin Co., 1925.

Giddings, F. H., *Scientific Study of Human Society*. Univ. of North Carolina Press, 1924.

Gide, C., and Rist, C., *Histoire des doctrines economiques depuis les Physiocrates jusqu'a nos jours*. J. B. Sirey, Paris, 1909.

Gillin, J. L., *Poverty and Dependency*. The Century Co., 1921. *Criminology and Penology*. The Century Co., 1926.

Gleason, A. H., *What the Workers Want*. Harcourt, Brace & Co., 1920.

Gras, N. S. B., *Introduction to Economic History*. Harper & Brothers, 1922.

Hamilton, W. H. (ed.), *Current Economic Problems*. Rev. ed., Univ. of Chicago Press, 1919.

Hetherington, H. J. W., and Muirhead, J. H., *Community Life and Civic Problems*. Ginn & Co., 1922.

Hobhouse, L. T., *Social Evolution and Political Theory*. Lemcke, 1911. *Social Development*. Henry Holt & Co., 1924.

Hobson, J. A., *Work and Wealth*. Macmillan, 1914. *Free Thought in the Social Sciences*. Macmillan, 1926.

Hoxie, R. F., *Scientific Management and Labor*. D. Appleton & Co., 1915. *Trade Unionism in the United States*. D. Appleton & Co., 1923.

Israel, H., and Landis, B. Y., *Handbook of Social Resources*. Univ. of Chicago Press, 1926.

Jenks, J., and Lauck, W. J., *The Immigration Problem*. Funk & Wagnalls, 1912.

Judd, C. H., *Psychology of Social Institutions*. Macmillan, 1926.

Kallen, H. M., *Education, the Machine, and the Worker*. Republic Publishing Co., 1925.

Kellar, A. G., *Starting-Points in Social Science*. Ginn & Co., 1925.

Kellor, F. A., *Immigrants in America*. N. Y. Committee for Immigrants in America, 1915.

Kelsey, Carl, *Physical Basis of Society*. D. Appleton & Co., 1916.

King, I., *Education for Social Efficiency*. D. Appleton & Co., 1915.

Laguna, Theodore de, *Factors of Social Evolution*. Crofts, 1926.

McDougall, William, *Introduction to Social Psychology*. Luce, 1916.

MacIver, R. M., *Elements of Social Science*. E. P. Dutton & Co., 1921. *Community: A Sociological Study*. New ed., Macmillan, 1924.

McMahon, T. S., *Social and Economic Standards of Living*. D. C. Heath, 1925.

Marshall, L. C., *Story of Human Progress*. Macmillan, 1925. (Ed.), *Readings in Industrial Society*. Univ. of Chicago Press, 1918.

Mowrer, E. R., *Family Disorganization*. Univ. of Chicago Press, 1927.

Odum, H. W., *American Masters of Social Science*. Henry Holt & Co., 1927.

Ogburn, W. F., *Social Change with Respect to Culture and Original Nature*. Huebsch, 1922.

Overstreet, H. A., *Influencing Human Behavior*. People's Institute, 1925.

Park, R. E., and others, *The City*. Univ. of Chicago Press, 1925.

Park, R. E., and Burgess, E. W., *Introduction to the Science of Sociology*. Univ. of Chicago Press, 1924.

Parker, C. H., *Casual Laborer*. Harcourt, Brace & Co., 1920.

Parmelee, M. F., *Science of Human Behavior*. Macmillan, 1913.

Parsons, E. W., *Social Freedom: A Study of the Conflicts Between Social Classifications and Personality*. G. P. Putnam's Sons, 1915.

Parsons, P. A., *Introduction to Modern Social Problems*. Alfred A. Knopf, 1924.

Pearson, Karl, *Grammar of Science*. W. Scott, Ltd., London, 1895.

Peixotto, J. B., *Control of Poverty*. Univ. of California, 1923. *Getting and Spending at the Professional Standard of Living*. Macmillan, 1927.

Pigou, A. C., *Wealth and Welfare*. Macmillan, 1912. *Economics of Welfare*. New ed., Macmillan, 1925.

Pipkin Charles W., *Idea of Social Justice*. Macmillan, 1926.

Platt, Charles, *Psychology of Social Life*. Dodd, Mead & Co., 1922.

Queen, S. A., and Mann, D. M., *Social Pathology*. Thomas Y. Crowell Co., 1925.

Randall, J. H., *The Making of the Modern Mind*. Houghton Mifflin Co., 1926.

Richmond, M. E., *The Good Neighbor in the Modern City*. J. B. Lippincott Co., 1907.

Robinson, J. H., *Mind in the Making*. Harper & Brothers, 1921. *Ordeal of Civilization*. Harper & Brothers, 1926.

Ross, E. A., *Principles of Sociology*. The Century Co., 1920. *Social Trend*. The Century Co., 1922.

Rowntree, B. S., *Human Factor in Business*. Longmans, Green & Co., 1925.

Rowntree, H., *Changing Human Nature*. The Stratford Co., 1923.

Rubinow, I. M., *Social Insurance*. Henry Holt & Co., 1913.

Russell, Bertrand, *Political Ideals*. The Century Co., 1917. *Proposed Roads to Freedom*. Henry Holt & Co., 1919. *Education and the Good Life*. Boni & Liveright, 1926.

Russell, Bertrand, and D. W., *Prospects of Industrial Civilization*. The Century Co., 1923.

Russell, H. A., *New Socialism*. Shakespeare Press, 1916.

Salomon, Alice, *Soziale Diagnose*. Heymanns, Berlin, 1926.

Schweitzer, A., *Philosophy of Civilization*. 2v. Macmillan, 1923.

Seager, H. R., *Social Insurance*. Macmillan, 1910.

Sechrist, F. K., *Education and the General Welfare*. Macmillan, 1920.

Shearman, H. P., *Practical Economics*. McGraw, 1922.

Siegfried, André, *America Comes of Age*. Harcourt, Brace & Co., 1927.

Small, Albion W., *Origins of Sociology*. Univ. of Chicago Press, 1924.

Snowden, Philip, *Socialism and Syndicalism*. Warwick & York, 1915.

Sorokin, Pitirim, *The Sociology of Revolution*. J. B. Lippincott Co., 1925.

Spargo, John, *Syndicalism, Industrial Unionism, and Socialism*. Huebsch, 1913. *Social Democracy Explained*. Harper & Brothers, 1919.

Spencer, A. G., *Woman's Share in Social Culture*. (2d ed.) J. B. Lippincott & Co., 1925.

Sumner, W. G., and Keller, A. G., *Science of Society*. 4v. Yale Univ. Press, 1927.

Tawney, R. H., *Acquisitive Society*. Harcourt, Brace & Co., 1920.

Thomas, E., *Industry, Emotion, and Unrest*. Harcourt, Brace & Co., 1920.

Thomas, F., *Environmental Basis of Society*. The Century Co., 1925.

Thomas, J. H., *When Labour Rules*. Harcourt, Brace & Co., 1921.

Thomson, G. H., *Instinct, Intelligence, and Character.* Longmans, Green & Co., 1925.

Thrasher, F. M., *The Gang.* Univ. of Chicago Press, 1926.

Tridon, A., *The New Unionism.* Huebsch, 1913.

Tugwell, R. G., *American Industry Comes of Age.* Harcourt, Brace & Co., 1927. *Essays in Economic Theory.* With an introduction by H. R. Seager. Alfred A. Knopf, 1924.

Vandervelde, E., *Socialism versus the State.* Kerr, 1919.

Van Waters, Miriam, *Youth in Conflict.* Republic Publishing Co., 1925.

Veblen, T. B., *The Instinct of Workmanship and the State of the Industrial Arts.* Huebsch, 1914. *Place of Science in Modern Civilization.* Huebsch, 1919. *Theory of Business Enterprise.* Charles Scribner's Sons, 1921.

Wallas, Graham, *The Great Society.* Macmillan, 1914.

Walling, W. E., and others (eds.), *Socialism of Today.* Henry Holt & Co., 1916.

Warbasse, J. P., *Coöperative Democracy Attained Through Voluntary Association of the People as Consumers.* Macmillan, 1923.

Ward, H. F., *The New Social Order.* Macmillan, 1919.

Ward, L. F., *Dynamic Sociology; or Applied Social Science as Based Upon Statical Sociology and the Less Complex Sciences.* D. Appleton & Co., 1910.

Warne, F. J., *Tide of Immigration.* D. Appleton & Co., 1916.

Watson, J. B., *Psychology.* J. B. Lippincott & Co., 1918.

Watts, Frank, *Introduction to Psychological Problems of Industry.* Allen (London), 1921.

Weatherly, U. G., *Social Progress.* J. B. Lippincott & Co., 1926.

Webb, Sidney and Beatrice, *Decay of Capitalist Civilization*. Harcourt, Brace & Co., 1923.

Wells, H. G., *Social Forces in England and America*. Harper & Brothers, 1914. *Salvaging of Civilization*. Macmillan, 1921. *Year of Prophesying*. Macmillan, 1925.

Wells, L. R., *Industrial History of the United States*. Macmillan, 1922.

Weyl, W. E., *The New Democracy*. Macmillan, 1912.

Whitehead, A. N., *Science and the Modern World*. Macmillan, 1926.

Wilde, N., *Ethical Basis of the State*. Princeton Univ. Press, 1924.

Williams, F. E., and others, *Social Aspects of Mental Hygiene*. Yale Univ. Press, 1925.

Williams, Whiting, *What's on the Worker's Mind?* Charles Scribner's Sons, 1920.

Wines, F. H., *Punishment and Reformation*. Thomas Y. Crowell Co., 1919.

Wissler, Clark, *Man and Culture*. Thomas Y. Crowell Co., 1923.

Withers, H., *Case for Capitalism*. E. P. Dutton & Co., 1920.

Wolfe, A. B., *Conservatism, Radicalism, and Scientific Method*. Macmillan, 1923.

Woolf, L. S., *Coöperation and the Future of Industry*. Macmillan, 1919.

Wright, H. W., *Moral Standards of Democracy*. D. Appleton & Co., 1925.

Yeaxlee, B. A., *Spiritual Values in Adult Education*. Oxford University Press, 1925.

Yerkes, R. M., and La Rue, D. W., *Materials for a Study of the Self*. 2d ed., Harvard Univ. Press, 1914.

Zimand, S., *Modern Social Movements*. H. W. Wilson, 1921.

Periodical Articles and Pamphlets

Barnes, H. E., "The Fate of Sociology in England." *Publications of the American Sociological Society,* XXI, 26-46. Univ. of Chicago Press, 1927.

Blackmar, F. W., "The Sociology Complex," *Journal of Applied Sociology,* X, 203-12.

Eklund, E. G., "The Normal Family," *The Survey,* LVI, 628-29.

Eubank, E. E., "The Concepts of Sociology," *Social Forces,* V, 386-400.

Gehlke, C. E., "The Use and Limitations of Statistics in Sociological Research," *American Sociological Society,* XXI, 141-48. Univ. of Chicago Press, 1927.

Gillin, J. L., "The Development of Sociology in the United States," *ibid.,* pp. 1-25.

Hart, Hornell, "Science and Sociology," *American Journal of Sociology,* XXVII, 364-82.

Karpf, F. B., "The Development of Social Psychology," *American Sociological Society,* XXI, 71-81. Univ. of Chicago Press, 1927.

Marshall, L. C., "How May We Foster or Facilitate the Development of the Social Sciences?" *Journal of Political Economy,* Vol. XXXV, No. 2.

Merriam, C. E., "Progress in Political Research," *American Political Science Review,* Vol. XX, No. 1.

Mitchell, W. C., "Quantitative Analysis in Economic Theory," *American Economic Review,* Vol. XV, No. 1.

INDEX